THE WORLD'S BEST NETWORK
MARKETING STRATEGIES

BY: ROB SPERRY

THE WORLD'S BEST NETWORK
MARKETING STRATEGIES

BY: ROB SPERRY

TGON Publishing

TGON Publishing

© 2022 TGON Publishing. All Rights Reserved

Reproduction or translation of any part of this book beyond that permitted by Section 107 or 108 of the 1976 United States Copyright Act without written permission of the copyright owner is unlawful. Criminal copyright infringement is investigated by the FBI and may constitute a felony with a maximum penalty of up to five years in prison and/or a $250,000 fine. Request for permission or further information should be addressed to TGON Publishing.

Warning—Disclaimer

The purpose of this book is to educate and inspire. This book is not intended to give advice or make promises or guarantees that anyone following the ideas, tips, suggestions, techniques or strategies will have the same results as the people listed throughout the stories contained herein. The author, publisher and distributor(s) shall have neither liability nor responsibility to anyone with respect to any loss or damage caused, or alleged to be caused, directly or indirectly by the information contained in this book.

CONTENTS

INTRODUCTION　　9

1　ALICIA WILLIAMS　　13

2　AMBER BRILL　　25

3　ASHLYN MILLANG　　35

4　BRENDA GEIGER　　45

5　CHRISTIAAN J. PETERS　　55

6　DEBRAISHA TONEY-HALE　　65

7　HEATHER BAUMAN　　75

8　JENNIFER PIPER KENNEDY　　85

9　JENNIFER STROMAN　　97

10　JUSTINE LAYSER　　109

11　LESLEY WEISS ZWICK　　123

12　LISA S. HILL　　133

13	LAURA CAROFFINO	143
14	LORI BENSON	153
15	MISS MARILYN	161
16	MORGAN ZAMBRANO	171
17	RANDY CHRISTOPHER	181
18	RHONDA ARZA	191
19	SANDY HUMPEL	201
20	SONIA LINE ARSENEAU	207
21	SUE BRENCHLEY	217

CONCLUSION 227

"When you are ignorant in a subject, start educating yourself by finding an expert in the field or a book on the subject."

— Robert T. Kiyosaki

INTRODUCTION

I remember when I said yes to my first network marketing company. Right before I joined I was contemplating if this really was the right decision for me and my family. I had been approached multiple times before by different people in different network marketing companies. But there was one big difference this time. The big difference was the person who asked me. I had looked up to this man for a long time and had always wanted to be mentored by him.

We had known each other personally, and I was always impressed by him. He had a way of connecting that I had never experienced before, and I just kept thinking that there was something different about him that I liked and wanted to know more about. It didn't matter what the product or the company was, because I wanted this guy to be my mentor. Lucky for me, it turned out the company and product were stellar, but it was because of my mentor that I learned how to sell anything to anyone.

I have since retired from working in specific network marketing companies, and now I dedicate my life to helping people as a generic network marketing coach. I specialize in hosting masterminds that range from people just starting out to seven and eight-figure earners. I also do private coaching, have been a keynote speaker around the world, written a dozen books, and host a variety of communities for people in the network marketing industry. I am passionate about helping people be successful in their network marketing businesses.

With all of this experience in network marketing myself and helping thousands of people with their businesses, I know one thing for sure; you need a mentor! I don't care where you are at in your business, if you don't have a mentor or a coach, you are putting yourself in more stressful situations, and going to struggle more than you would if you had a mentor or a coach.

Whenever you start something new, you are met with feelings of excitement, anxiousness, and maybe even some fear. We get caught up in HOW we are going to be successful in the new venture instead of focusing on our mindset. I like to call this "HOW greed" and we are all guilty of it. We think that if we know the HOW, then those feelings of fear or anxiousness will go away. I watch people come to me with the "HOW greed" all of the time. "How do I do videos on social media?" "How do I get people interested in my product?" "How do I tell my story without sounding salesy?" The HOW greed list could go on and on.

Now you may be sitting there thinking, "YES! I want to know the answer too!" I have some hard truth for you, and I want you to listen up. It's not the "HOW" that you need, it's the mindset and the belief that is missing. Getting the right mentors in your corner is going to help you learn the mindset and belief, and don't worry...we will give you the tools and actions steps too!

We all face fears when we start something new. I know that one of the best ways I conquer my fear is to get the right mentors on my team.

INTRODUCTION

Whether I was learning how to do network marketing, or learning the art of tennis, the very best thing I always do to ensure my success is to get people who have already been successful in the area I am focusing on and study them. If you picked up this book, chances are you are new to network marketing. "New" could mean this is your very first network marketing business. It could also mean that you are on a new team, or perhaps you are jumping back into a network marketing business that you have had for quite some time.

Regardless of where you are in network marketing, this book is going to be an asset for you. I have compiled some of the best people in network marketing to write chapters for this book. These are your mentors. They are your coaches. They are going to share with you tips, stories, and systems that helped them become successful in their network marketing business. They are going to share with you the best network marketing strategies that will help grow your business if you listen and apply what they are teaching you.

I was thrilled to see how dedicated each of these authors was to sharing the most valuable content with you. They are also going to share with you some of their stories about where they were before network marketing. I want to encourage you to pay attention to each author. In order to know where you want to go, you first have to know where you are at. We have created this book to give you the guidance and direction that you need as you start or continue in network marketing. Each chapter has been written by a different leader in network marketing. Every chapter starts with a list of accomplishments that each individual has had. Make sure to check those out! We have some experience, expertise and downright legends who are contributing to this book. I have added some of my own thoughts and teaching throughout each chapter in the "COACH`S NOTES" sections. Be willing to take notes and remember to take action quickly! Let`s get started.

"No one is you, and that is your SUPERPOWER!"

— Unknown

ALICIA WILLIAMS

- Native of Alabama currently residing in Georgia with her husband and three children. One daughter and two sons. Has been in network marketing for ten years.

- Former Educator who retired herself before the age of 40 from a 15-year career in the field after only two years in the business.

- Top .01 percent in her company, six-figure earner award for FIVE consecutive years.

- Leads a team of over 100,000 consultants.

- Signature necklace, "The Alicia" named in her honor.

- First African American Elite Leader in her company. She shares hope and empowers her team to walk in their own greatness.

5 Effective Ways To Stay Motivated and Win On Purpose

I am pretty sure that William Shakespeare was talking about me when he boldly wrote, "And though she be little, she is fierce!" If you can believe in yourself, you will become unstoppable at whatever you decide to accomplish. Everything that I have set out to achieve on this journey started with the choice to BELIEVE in myself.

One of my careers was as a college program director on a very well-known college campus. As the youngest person who had ever done this job, I was immediately looked at by my now fellow peers, who were much older, as unworthy or undeserving of such a position. There was no one to turn to that saw me as deserving or that believed in me. I was forced to find my voice and believe that I did deserve it. I knew I was qualified and that I was the right person for the role. I had to have my own back and know that I believed in ME and no one else mattered. In this chapter, you will learn how to stay motivated and win on purpose even when others doubt who you are and what you can achieve.

#1 What's Your Superpower?

"No one is you and that is your Superpower."

– Unknown

Knowing who you are and whose you are matters. We are all wonderfully and fearfully made. We are all capable of our own unique contributions to this world. Who are you? What sets you apart from everyone else? You must identify the intangible skills that set you apart from the rest of this world. These skills could be for example as follows: strong WORK ethic, a person of high integrity, or being a person who keeps their word. It is important that you know for yourself who you are and what sets you apart.

There will always be someone better or, smarter than you, but NO one is YOU! Surround yourself with others who see greatness in you and who will push you to level up. But, as I mentioned before, the most important thing is that you see greatness in yourself first. Greatness looks different for all of us. Some of us may have amazing listening skills, or the ability to believe in others. Someone else may have the gift of sales and motivating people. Don't focus on what skills you don't have. Don't focus your attention on trying to be the next Michael Jordan or Kobe Bryant in your industry, but instead be the next YOU. Be yourself and know that YOU are your own superpower.

As a former educator, teaching is a work of heart. Many have been blessed with the gift to inspire and empower others to greatness. It is an educator's superpower. When my students wanted to give up or throw in the towel, I stepped in with words of encouragement letting them know that nothing was impossible for those who believe. I remember seeing one student, in particular, that was struggling. I knew that he had the capability to be more and do more, but he was showing up lacking the confidence and motivation to see his potential. I saw him wanting to give up on himself and that just wouldn't cut it for him. I sat him down and gave him a glimpse of what I saw in him. I gave him the bigger picture, not just a test score on a sheet of paper. That changed everything for him. The way this confidence shot through the roof after that conversation was life-changing for him, and for me. Up to this point, I hadn't seen that I had a superpower. I had just thought that I cared and was passionate about what I was doing. But when I watched this particular student grow and change that was when I knew what my superpower was. I was incredible at inspiring and empowering others to believe in themselves.

As an entrepreneur, knowing and identifying your strengths (superpower) will push or carry you through when the tough times arise. We often see the good in others and can identify their strengths, but we can struggle to see our own. It is so important that you take the time to see what your superpowers are. Although some will encourage you, it will be ultimately up to you to always know your strengths and to work on nurturing them. In this industry, your success is totally up to you. The harsh reality is no one is coming to save you. You must do the saving all on your own. You must posture up, believe that it`s possible, put on your cape, and go get it!

Coach's Notes: Alicia nailed it. "Knowing and identifying your strengths (superpower) will push or carry you through when the tough times arise." This sentence summed up so much. First off, notice how Alicia said WHEN rather than IF. Tough times will arise. Next, she understands that we have our most success from our strengths. Double down on those strengths and make them even better because they are what makes you unique.

#2 Mindset Matters-Adopting a Champion Mindset

"The mind is everything.
What you think you become."

– Buddha

Can you see it? Can you see yourself succeeding and creating the life of your dreams? Can you see yourself walking the stage to receive the award you got from your company? Can you see yourself helping to change the lives of others around you? Before you accomplish anything, you must first see yourself as a success. In the network marketing industry, many have doubted if they could have the success they desire. They will start to doubt if they made the right choice by choosing to sign up with a company. Or, maybe you wonder if the product you are selling is really what you want to be selling and if this is the right choice for you. Have you ever said to yourself, "Oh boy what did I get myself into?"

You may even let other people and their opinions and judgments get into your head. The Negative Nancy and the Bad Attitude Bob tell you that it is not possible, and you start to believe them! This happens! But you have to come back to yourself and remember that you said yes to this opportunity and network marketing for a reason. You ultimately believe in the brand, the vision, and the products. It doesn`t matter what other people think or say. Your passion will be contagious to others when you remind yourself and start to act from your superpowers. This burning passion or desire will push you to no limits to believing you can achieve your dreams and goals.

Over the years, I`ve pushed for next-level rank advancements and company incentive trips. I have achieved many, but have also fallen short with some. One of the biggest lessons I have learned from all of my experiences was to never throw the towel in too fast. Fight until the end. Some of my biggest accomplishments happened in the eleventh hour. If I would have given up when I thought it was going to work out, I would be guaranteeing that I would reach the goal. Not throwing the towel in too fast enabled me to work hard and go all-in on myself. This is a champion`s mindset. The race is not given to the swift or strong, but to the one who endures to the end. In your network marketing business, you will experience failure after failure, after failure. In these times you are not losing, you are learning.

Success in network marketing is a journey. On this journey, you must have heart. Prepare for the heartbreaks, disappointments, lack of support, and setbacks. When others give up on you, just make sure you don`t give up on yourself. If at first, you don`t succeed, pick yourself up and try again. Get back on the front line and give it all you got. No one said it would be easy, it's worth it. You are worth it. Your family is worth it!

The victory in network marketing is having the mindset of a champion. Believing in yourself even when no one else does.

#3 The Power of Your Story

"In order to win a man to your cause, you must first reach his heart, the great high road to his reason."

– Abraham Lincoln

As you often heard before, people don't buy products, they buy people. You can no longer tell people how you made it happen, you must show them. Who are you? What do you have to offer them? In the words of Tom Cruise, "show me the money"! They simply want to know how they can get to the money and get it fast. As Zig Ziglar says, "there's no elevator to success, you must take the stairs."

People connect with people who inspire or motivate them through similar life experiences. What were your struggles, and hardships? What sacrifices did you make along the way? How did you push past the pain? Facts tell, but stories sell and connect to the masses. If you want others to connect you must connect with them by being your authentic self. Don't be ashamed of your story, it will inspire others. Ever read someone's story and think, " This is exactly what I needed to hear today?" Your story will do that for someone else.

I often think of my early years in my current company. At times, I was ashamed or somewhat embarrassed to share what I was currently doing on the side in network marketing, and I had to supplement my income to feed my shopping habit. I dare not wear this as a professional, let alone sell it. Although my salary was not bad at all, within the first two years of being with this company I was able to retire from my career of 15 years. My message to you is to never be ashamed of your side hustle, no one is going to feed you if you go broke.

Don`t allow others to downplay what you`re doing. Share your story, it`s bigger than you. Someone is counting on you. Be a beacon of light and inspiration to others, a hope dealer. We know many are skeptics of our industries, however being transparent by sharing your story, and your humble beginnings and showing up as your authentic self will connect you with the right individuals.

Coach's Notes: One of the biggest cliches in network marketing is that facts tell and stories sell. It is 100% true and will always be true. We love a good movie or book because of the story it tells. All too often network marketers skip this vital step of improving their communication/storytelling. I can tell you based on experience that storytelling was a major weakness of mine. It took me years of focus and paying attention to other great storytellers to learn how to tell a better story. I felt uncomfortable showing emotion. I left out the important details. I also felt that I didn't have a powerful story. That is never true. Each one of you has a very powerful story. You just need to learn how to tell it which will come from deliberate practice.

#4 Your Are Your Own Competition

"Comparison is the thief of joy."

— Theodore Roosevelt

Look in the mirror... that's your competition. It's you vs. you. Your only focus is being better than the person you were yesterday. Your journey to achieving your goals or having the success that you desire is your race at your pace. You can't compare your Chapter 3 to someone else's Chapter 33. Your vision and goals may align with others, but your journey will be different.

My ten years of networking marketing have taught me to stay in my lane with a focus on helping others to achieve their goals. This industry is designed so that we all can win. You can outrank your upline, or your team members can outrank you. I have been on both sides of surpassing my upline in rank, but have also had team members within my downline outrank me too. It is one of the best parts of network marketing. Your journey to success is your own and not paced by someone else.

On your journey to success in this industry, your competition is procrastination, your ego, the knowledge you neglect, a negative mindset, and your lack of creativity. Compete against that.

It's never about being the best, it's about being better than who you were yesterday. Bet on you!

#5 The SWSWSWSW Philosophy

"Don't worry about being successful but work towards being significant and the success will naturally follow."

— *Oprah Winfrey*

Entrepreneurship is not for the faint at heart.

Network Marketing is not for everyone, but everyone can do it.

Building a business can be tough and you will inevitably encounter rejection and disappointment from prospects, team members, and family and friends. Don`t trip and don`t definitely quit. Take a breather and remember:

Some Will
Some Won`t
So What
Show up and Work

Coach's Notes: I absolutely love this phrase that Alicia shared.
Some Will
Some Won't
So What
Show up and Work

This phrase gives us more perspective on the process of success which ultimately leads to success. All too often we focus solely on results. Yes, results can be an indicator but they aren't the only indicator. For example, if you sign up five people next week and they all quit are you bad at network marketing? Let's go further. Let's say after they quit you don't get any better but the following week you sign up for just one person. That one person then goes and signs up ten people in the business. Are you better or worse than you were the week before? You are exactly the same but based on the results you think you are better or worse. Managing your emotions is one of the biggest keys to success in network marketing.

Stop trying to convince people that this is the opportunity for them. Don't tell, show them. Take them on your journey often to show how this business is impacting your life positively and your team members. Show the fun and exciting things happening. Ignore the noise of the naysayers and dream busters. Focus your time and energy on those who are happy for you and inspire, and motivate you to continue to grow.

Dear Entrepreneur,

You've entered the fastest growing business model, Network Marketing. This is your season to walk in your greatness! Be confident and believe in who you are, fight for what you desire, inspire others through your journey, compete with no one but yourself, and stay positive through it all.

Let's Go, Grow and Glow!

ALICIA WILLIAMS

> *"Be the change you wish to see in the world."*
>
> *— Mahatma Gandhi*

AMBER BRILL

- Full-time network marketer with multiple 7-figure online businesses.
- Earned 17 free trips through a 15-year career.
- Personally recruited over 1,000 business partners.
- Coached and developed multiple 6-figure earners.
- Featured in several publications.
- Current network marketing business has over 30,000 customers and 1,700 team members.

Shifting and changing

I started over fifteen years ago in a party planning company in the network marketing industry. My main goal when I started was to do something fun to get out of the house. I was a new stay-at-home mom with a precious baby girl. While I loved being at home with her, I missed the interaction with people all day that I had in my corporate job. Now, don't get me wrong, I loved being home and not missing a single moment in my baby girl's life; I just missed the adults that could talk with me. Money wasn't why I got started; I just wanted fun and people. I found a company doing at-home purse parties on Craigslist and decided to join up. At the time, I would have never imagined that this fun thing I was doing to get out of the house would turn into a full-time income.

Life has an interesting way of shifting and changing. Five years ago, I found myself in a challenging position. My previous network marketing company wasn't going well. I found myself a single mom in my personal life after recently divorcing. I couldn't pay my bills, even though I worked 60 hours a week. I was embarrassed to talk about what I thought was a complete disaster in life and business. My closest friends and family didn't even know what I was going through. It felt too big and embarrassing to admit, but now I realize how many people go through something similar to what I did. I realized that when I shared my struggles with others, I was in a position to help others move forward in their own lives. But to do that, I had to overcome my fears of being embarrassed and feeling judged. I am so glad that I did. I started making empowering decisions for my own life and creating the change that I needed to succeed. The very best part for me is that I can inspire others to keep going and make their wildest dreams come true as well.

Your reasons for doing this business will change over time. It can change from wanting to have fun and talking to people, to needing a full-time income that can support you and your family. I fell in love with the industry for what it did for me being a stay-at-home mom. I quickly realized that network marketing could become a lot more than just a hobby. Network marketing was an opportunity to change my life, my future, and build a business and the income that would help me empower and help other people do the same.

Your story will not always be the same. As you reach milestones in your career, your story will change, and you will end up with multiple layers of your story to share to increase the impact on your audience based on where they are in their life.

Coach's Notes: Does your why make you cry? When I first started, my why hadn't been found. I felt a little guilty thinking about what is wrong with me. As my time in the business grew, so did my why and purpose. Eventually it became clear, but I always had to be open to things shifting and changing. Change is inevitable. The most important thing is how you deal with it.

Stand out from the crowd

There are so many people online with businesses; it's really important to stand out and be yourself. The ultimate goal is to stand out online and make a huge positive impact with a ripple effect for millions. You want to share the good, the bad, and the ugly guys. You may read this and think, "Oh yeah, but Amber doesn't mean it." Let me say it again. Share the good, the bad, AND the ugly. Sharing is what makes excellent connections with others. No one lives in the "Instagram Life," where everything is vacations, parties, and epic experiences. Sharing my story has helped me create a legacy for my family. I've turned my mess into my message, and have helped so many others create a path towards improving their lives by doing the same. Never be afraid to share the struggles and less-than-perfect moments of your life. But more importantly, what you did to navigate your way through those struggles, to find yourself in a better place on the other side.

Social media can be such a powerful tool and impactful in people's lives when used in the right way. The problem with social media these days is that so many focus on the highlights of their lives and paint a picture, showing their best moments. That's often viewed as unrealistic to their audience. We can use social media every day through life's highs and the lows. So why not showcase everything in your life to make an impact and allow your story to help others succeed and overcome their struggles as well? Showing the glamorous life and not telling them how you got there and the struggles you had to overcome doesn't provide any benefit or value to your audience. Studies show that social media can often influence people in a negative way, leading others to feel down about themselves, and as if everyone has a better life than you do. It's always been a really important goal for me to keep my social media authentic, honest, fun, helpful, and never try to paint a picture-perfect life because, really does one even exist?

I often show up messy with my baby in tow, the puppy biting us, and a teenager that is, well, a teenager. But I humbly share my story of where I was, what changes I made, and how I showed up consistently to build the empire I'm so blessed to have. I also share how I got to the point of my life and created the success that I always desired, to have the money to do what I want when I want, and the time freedom to do the things with my family and make those memories.

I pour into others daily to uplift them, breathe life, and let them know that their past does not define them. I share the message that their present does not determine their future and that anything is possible with hard work, determination, a good attitude, and consistency. Creating a powerful story that's relatable to many is the key to standing out on social media. Your story has the power to impact millions of lives if you are sharing all of it. This can be done with a simple strategy beginning with where you came from and what was your struggle. After that, let your audience know how you overcame that struggle. Lastly, what was your end result? Everyone has a story, and we should be able to share that story with the world to relate, inspire and empower.

Coach's Notes: Standing out from the crowd was hard for me the first few years in network marketing. I was so scared that I didn't even make one post on social media pertaining to anything alluding to network marketing, and this was even after I had hit the top ranks in the company. But here is what I learned and why Amber's last paragraph is so important. Attention is the #1 currency in marketing. Here is the key—attention with the right intention. I think of the people I look up to. Jesus Christ, Gandhi, Mother Teresa, and Martin Luther King Jr., Each one of them had to have some sort of attention in order to create the lasting impact they did. They all did it with the right intention.

Simple, short, and to the point

Our story should be told really in less than three minutes, short, simple, and to the point. The more powerful your story is, and the more often you tell it, the more lives you will impact. I suggest staying true to yourself, both in-person and online. Authenticity helps create an audience that knows, likes, and trusts you. If you are the same person online as you are in real life, people will respect that and want to get to know you. You never want to pretend to be someone that you are not or try to be someone else. Be you and attract the tribe that you desire.

When you first start this industry, it can sometimes be hard to let yourself be vulnerable and authentic. You may even be embarrassed by the current situation you're in or your past. I often hear many are worried about sharing their success story, afraid they will come off as bragging. I promise you this is not the case. I feel like that is a really big objection for new people to start sharing their stories, but I want you to know that whatever your struggles are and what you will overcome will help somebody else. When you share your true authentic self, it will speak to many, from your struggle to success. Staying humble is key and never forget where you came from.

I see many people in businesses that are constantly spamming their pages with products, and buy this, and buy that, which is not an effective strategy. People will do business with those they know, like, trust and who are relatable to them. So by sharing your story, maybe not only your business story of where you were before, how you got to where you are now, and what you've achieved, sharing a story of products is also important. If you can show someone the benefits of the product you are currently selling or marketing and how it will help their life, I feel like that is important.

I feel that it's important to share your story authentically, to be yourself both in-person and online. So, as you're sharing and being your authentic self, there's really no difference between sharing your story online or being in person. If you're sharing your story the same as you would when talking to your best friend in person, it will come across the same way whenever you're sharing it online. You can share your story by doing that in your social media posts, by doing in your actual stories, by doing reels, to share where you were, where you are now, how you overcame that to get to where you. So that way, as you're sharing and being your authentic self, you want to make sure that there's no difference in sharing your story online or sharing it in person. Authenticity is universal and translates wherever you are sharing.

Sharing my story has taken my business from being just a small business to make a little extra money, to help support bills, to building an online multimillion-dollar empire. It has not only impacted my life, but has impacted the lives of thousands of others by teaching them to share their story and be their authentic-self as well.

Network marketing has changed my life. I came here for a little extra money and found myself in a horrible position over five years ago. Now that I have a multi-million dollar business, I am now home with my children full time, and I've also been able to retire my fiancé. So both of us are home 24/7.

If you are just starting in this industry, I strongly advise sitting down and taking some time to figure out your goals, where you want to be, and where you see yourself in three, five or ten years? How is this industry going to help you and impact the lives of others? What is the current struggle that you want to overcome? Maybe it's money, maybe it's confidence, or just to make an impact. Figure out what you were before, where you're starting now, and what you're going to do to get to where you want to be so your story can impact as many others as possible.

A great story contains conflict and pain. Start by sharing your background, then share the solution to the conflict or pain you struggled with. Then share how you feel about your future and how much of your life has changed.

Once you have your story nailed down, practice telling it, and do that often! The more you tell your story, the better you will become. The more excitement you will have in your voice and the bigger the impact you will make. You never know how your stories impact others until you share them daily.

If I can go from being a broke single mom to a successful online entrepreneur by sharing my story in a true and authentic way on social media, I know that you can too!

Coach's Notes: There was one part that hit home for me. Amber said, "I feel that it's important to share your story authentically and be yourself, both in-person and online. So, as you're sharing and being your authentic self, there's really no difference between sharing your story online or being in person." You may think this is common sense, but it isn't. When one tries to be someone else online, and it doesn't match them, things never end well. Your goal on social media is to do a good enough job of showing who you are to the point that if someone met you in person for the first time, they would feel like they already know you.

AMBER BRILL

> *"I'm a great believer in luck, and I find the harder I work, the more I have of it."*
>
> *—Thomas Jefferson*

ASHLYN MILLANG

- Multi-six-figure earner.
- Has led teams of thousands.
- She consistently hustles to achieve her company's starting bonuses.
- Loves training the field.
- Featured trainer at her company conferences.

How to Start a Business with Your Hair on Fire!

Whether you're brand new to the network marketing industry or just started with a new company, the principles are the same. When I left a multi-million dollar team to launch a new company, I started from scratch. My entire network from my former company was essentially out of reach. It was like I hadn't spent the last several years building a successful business. As my kids would say, from playing way too much Minecraft, I was basically a total "newb." Some people could have seen this negatively, but I decided to embrace it! I decided to go all-in on being the "newb," and I decided to think like one.

When you're new to the industry, you don't know what you don't know. You're excited to do the dang thing, and guess what?? Excitement can be one of your most powerful assets! When we get too wrapped up in facts and information, we can easily overthink things and lose confidence. So while you might feel like you're on fire with excitement but don't know much else, I say run with it! You don't have to stress about *not knowing everything* right this minute; I will give you two business basics and a bonus tip that will get you into daily activity and create a foundation for your new business.

Coach's Notes: I have had the privilege of coaching Ashlyn for several years. I know that she practices what she teaches. In the last paragraph, she mentioned that, "excitement can be one of the most powerful assets." She also made mention that you don't need to know everything. Those two lines alone are so important that an entire book could be written just about that simple concept. Our enthusiasm sells! "But Rob, I don't know all the details, so I can't sell." Wrong! As long as you know it works, you can surely sell. I don't fully understand how I switch my light on, and suddenly, there is light. I get the basics but not he details. I definitely can sell or share how amazing is. Do not ever forget the importance of having that citement and enthusiasm. It is your secret sauce.

alled "Network" Marketing for a reason.

g relationships might sound like something that is a natural Some people, like extroverts and those that are naturally sociable, may not realize they possess an envious skill. It is also a skill that can be developed. Those who are more introverted also enjoy our relationships, but we seek them less or in different ways. We like people too, but something in our brains says, "Nah, let's just keep to ourselves." I point out these differences to illustrate that no matter your personality leanings, expanding your network by building authentic connections requires being intentional. So, where to start?

A great lesson I've learned in this field is how valuable relationships are. You already have a network to nourish–friends, family, acquaintances that you haven't taken the time to get to know better. You don't realize how out of touch you are with people until you get excited to share a new opportunity and start to think about how long it's been since you caught up with some of your favorite people. I honestly had many regrets for letting life (and depression and anxiety) keep me in this little bubble where I didn't seek conversations and connections with others. Now I had a reason to, and the lack of foundation made it feel awkward. Let's unpack that, shall we?

Some of you also feel awkward while thinking of people you want to connect with but haven't in a while. I've just talked to you about nurturing relationships with people to expand your business-building skills. That might feel a little bit skeevy or maybe even unethical. If you're breathing a sigh of relief because I'm reading your mind, you can now relax. The difference between the spammy creeps and a rockstar like you is that you are acting with a little thing called INTENTION. Intention is the act of sharing to provide value.

An example is sharing a post about a common problem your product can solve or sharing additional tips related to your specific market that your audience can implement with no purchase at all. You INTEND to provide value to your audience with what you have to offer and what you are passionate about sharing. So while you are making it a priority or even your "job" to nourish current relationships and develop new ones, you also realize how important it is to be more consistent and intentional with people. I promise you will come to appreciate that you've put in the effort to widen your circle of support through friendship and cultivating a professional network. The benefits will go both ways–you'll find support where you didn't have it before, and you'll be placed into the lives of others who are blessed to have you in their times of joy and sorrow.

When I decided to pursue the network marketing industry as my re-entry to the "working world," I was a tired, depressed, and often joyless stay-at-home mom. Yes, I did love my role as a mom, and I found joy in my children, but we all know that being a parent is a thankless job. My identity basically melted into the couch as another episode of Paw Patrol played in the background. I was going through the motions of life. I know that many of you can relate to this. I talked to a few friends, and I had my family, but I felt alone. I didn't feel "connected" or like I was providing much value to the world beyond changing diapers, cooking, or doing laundry. I was yearning for a way to contribute to my family's finances while continuing to be home for my husband and kids.

My identity used to be firmly rooted in independence, earning a living and working. In one fell swoop, I lost all three. I wanted it all but felt like I was completely lost. I needed a way to regain myself and have dabbled a bit in college; I thought about network marketing, and I knew this would be how I could make it happen. Through network marketing, I could have it all, and I also gained things that I never knew I needed. I have gained friendship, support, and a community through actively seeking deeper relationships and a broader network of many overlapping communities of people that enrich my life in ways I couldn't have imagined. I am going to share with you an action plan so you can start creating a life where you, too, can have it all.

Remember that this is going to take time and consistency. A great way to start is to pick one thing from the action plan and work consistently on it for two weeks.

ACTION PLAN:

1. Start by making a list of your current warm market with whom you may want to share your new product or opportunity. Your warm market is the people in your life from your family, work, social circles, activities, etc., with whom you already have some level of rapport. Your company and upline will have guidance on how to reach out using their system for leads, scripts, product sharing, third-party validations, etc. Use their system and remember what I just said about relationships and networking! You will be leaps ahead of other "newbs" because you were reminded about the importance of relationships–in business and life. You know that intentionally connecting with others is an incredible skill that will enhance your life and those in your network. Whether a natural (extrovert) or a guarded (introvert like me) relationship builder, you are now proudly a true people person. You give as much or more than you get, bringing value to the world.

2. Begin being more visible on social media; people want to see and hear from you! Post more, use your stories, comment on others posts, and take it to Messenger. When I feel like I've gotten a little out of touch, it genuinely feels good to catch up with others and start connecting again. The great thing about this process on social media is that the almighty algorithm will help you! As you connect with people, it does its thing and leads you to others! You'll start seeing old friends, making new ones, and becoming visible to new audiences who might benefit from what you have. It can become networking on steroids if you keep at it as you expand your reach more and more. Now let's address that potential voice in your head...

Some of you may struggle with seeking attention. I GET IT. You will ask yourself questions like, "Who cares what I have to say?" "Who is even watching?" "Do I look stupid?" A very wise coach I know (Rob, duh) talks about how many of us see getting attention as a bad thing. We feel like asking people to look at us is selfish. It definitely can be by some people, but you aren't one of those people! Rob says we have to retrain ourselves to understand that attention with INTENTION is never a bad thing. If you intend to provide value to others by sharing something useful or sharing your opportunity and products that you know will help others, then you have good intentions.

A bonus lesson for you to learn along the way–it's not about you; it's about others. The more you seek to bring value to others, the more will come back to you. Call it karma, call it the law of attraction, call it to balance...but just know that seeking to serve is the way to go.

Coach's Notes: I love a good action plan! This plan clearly outlines exactly how you can build more and better relationships. My favorite part about networking isn't just the business aspect but everything else that comes out of it. There will be so many connections that create immense value. Last week, I reached out to my ten most influential friends and asked them this question. "Who do you know that I could help provide value to." Through this one question, I have already made some key connections. I am always focusing on increasing the quantity and quality of my network. As Ashlyn laid it out, social media is one of the best ways to reach more people.

Get it Together!

I love a good dad joke and the ole "Working hard or hardly working?" is not only a classic, but it`s a legitimate question for network marketers. We can spend endless time "working" when in fact we are mostly just scrolling, making graphics, or chatting with teammates but not focused on business. In a profession that touts the ability to gain time freedom, we can easily get off track and waste a lot of that free time. For those who work full-time, your time is limited and precious; learn to use it wisely. If you`re a stay-at-home parent like I am, you have plenty to do but little structure, and it`s imperative that you find a way to separate your business from everyday life.

I have always struggled with time management and as someone with ADHD and depression, using tools and systems to keep focused is the only way to truly excel. My usual method of winging it was only going to take me so far, and in fact, I have met my limitations many times. I spent a little too long on scroll patrol and realized I hadn`t connected with anyone, but now it`s time to make dinner. After a coaching call, I took too much time chatting with a team member and ran out of time to make the other calls. So many times, I`ve messed around with other tasks and missed out on the most important ones. Make a plan for your time and tasks, and feel truly free when spending time in other areas.

ACTION PLAN:

1. Block Scheduling is your friend. It helps you identify the time you have available, the time you must be present for other things, and shows just how much or how little you have. It gives you perspective so you can properly prioritize your time and tasks! Start from the time you wake up until you go to bed. Block off work, "getting ready time," dinner with family, appointments, etc. Identify the time intervals when you can give your business your

total focus. It might be thirty minutes or even an hour but make that time worthwhile. Then when you're doing anything else, you give that your full attention.

2. Set daily minimums. If you work full time, you will likely utilize the weekends, but let's imagine you dedicate focused time to your business five days a week. Since you will utilize block scheduling you will know exactly when you'll have time to work, but setting minimums will give you the "what" to do in that time. These minimums aren't "just" what you do. They are your personal required minimum daily tasks. So if your kid gets sick, your tire goes flat, the in-laws drop-in, etc., you are committed to doing these *every day*. As you grow, you may get more detailed and specific in your daily minimums, but for now, it's full speed ahead just talking to people. You're going to be working on building relationships already and expanding your network but specifically decide how many people per day you're going to reach out to about your product or opportunity. When I am in building mode, I set a minimum of as high as ten people a day to offer my opportunity. Maybe that makes you want to vomit, which is understandable. I promise it gets easier, and if this introvert can be a people person, you can too. So, maybe you start with one or two per day but do them NO MATTER WHAT. Decide how many opportunities reach outs, customer follow-ups, and personal connections you will make each day. Even if everything goes wrong in your day, do this.

Coach's Notes: I have found the biggest difference between those who are successful and those who aren't is FOCUS! To focus, you must follow both of these simple steps. We need structure. By time blocking, you create focus to get things done. By creating minimums, you start to create habits. These habits create win streaks, and those win streaks can change your entire identity into becoming great! Greatness begins with creating those win streaks!

Action=Confidence

There is no better way to build your business than just…do it! You will say the wrong thing. You will do the wrong thing. You will feel like other people are just lucky. Here's the secret…it doesn't matter. It doesn't matter what others are doing, and it doesn't matter if you mess up. Just keep going and keep doing. I think the definition of luck is when hard work meets opportunity.

I think back to the first months in a brand new company as that shy, introverted mom, but I knew I had something special. I can distinctly remember the times I was brave and made the call, brought up the subject, tried the event, sent the message, asked for the sale, or offered the opportunity. I can directly trace the success and lineage of my business through those brave moments. That's where that luck and hard work come together. You may never know what you missed from the times you played small, but keeping in action will make those times happen less.

One way to keep your mindset in the right place is to practice daily personal development. You're already reading this book; that's personal development! Ask your upline, mentor, or side teammates for suggestions of great books, podcasts, or live training you can read, watch or listen to. Continually feeding your mind will sharpen your skills and keep you in action mode. Just make sure you apply the things you learn and utilize the two skills I shared above. Don't let the idea of soaking in knowledge keep you from doing income-producing activities.

I know you will doubt yourself based on what's happening around you. You can't help it, and it's a natural reaction. What you can do is keep going. Action is your number one defense against fear, comparison, and doubt. Staying in action will keep you moving forward, so even when you're feeling like you're doing all the things and not getting results, you are controlling the only thing you really can control…YOUR ACTIONS.

*"In our world,
the sky isn't even the limit."*

-Alpha Femme

BRENDA GEIGER

- Multiple 6 figure earner.

- Former Beauty Professional helping others in the industry stop exchanging time for money.

- Non-Profit President and Founder.

- Created multiple social media communities with thousands of women.

- Currently working with award winning international sale high level performance coach.

- Founder of Unbecoming Beta brand.

Let`s start out this chapter with some vulnerable honesty. I have barely written more than a Facebook status in the last ten years. Yet here I am as a co-author of a network marketing book with other powerhouses in the industry. Self-doubt has definitely reared its ugly head, and imposter syndrome has set in big time. But, that is no reason to stop or say no when incredible opportunities come our way. I continue to remind myself of the experiences I have had, the incredible accomplishments I have created, and that I absolutely have something to share that will be of value to you.

I am a badass with my craft. I have generated multiple six-figures in the last couple of years without having to step foot into an office or ask for a single day off. I have learned how to utilize and make money using free platforms that are available to all, but so many people don`t take advantage of them. I`ve learned to dance with the changes in the industry and shifted my strategies to complement the evolution of what we know as social media today. In this chapter, I am going to focus on Facebook, but understand the strategies and truths that I share will work with whatever social platform you decide to use for your business.

Congratulations on taking the initiative to be coachable and for investing in yourself! Throughout this book, you will have learned techniques that will help you collapse time so you do not have to fail forward as many times. We, as authors, are here to help accelerate your business goals quicker. As you read this chapter, I want to invite you into my mind and heart and take you behind the scenes of the art of building a social media account that is congruent to your brand.

I want you to think of your social media as your unique fingerprint. It is a social resume of your past and present that will potentially set you up for the future. It can be your virtual connection to loved ones and strangers worldwide. Grab your favorite beverage, get comfortable, and get ready to dig into the science behind one of our most significant business resources.

Coach's Notes: But don't leaders have it all figured out? They aren't ever scared? Brenda, thanks for starting out with the vulnerability. I have had multiple conversations with Brenda about her worries with writing her chapter, and you will all be glad she did once you read through it. Just remember that being scared is part of the process to success. Brenda, like all leaders, still has fears. The greatest difference between her and the unsuccessful is that she is willing to hit those fears head on. That example and piece of advice is more important than any skill we will ever learn. If we don't face those fears no amount of skill will ever compensate for our lack of deliberate action.

The Foundation

If you are anything like me, you have probably scrolled back on your own timeline to see what you used to post about. Or maybe you have had one of the notifications come up that says, "Look back four years ago." That is followed by pictures or your posts from four years ago. I remember the day that I first learned how to search my own timeline. I spent a good hour looking back, and one question kept popping into my head, "How in the world did I get here from there?" I couldn't believe that here I was, a six-figure earner that was crushing life, but there I was, reading posts I made in the past that would definitely lead me to have success. I became obsessed with reverse engineering and figuring out what my evolution in the online space had been. I found one key element when I started to investigate my own timeline. The foundation of a great business in your network.

We all have people that we connect with online. Most of those people, in the beginning, are going to be people you personally know. Friends and family, or people that you knew in your past. As you start to use social media more impactfully, we want to start to think more about our network and why we are connecting with them on social media. Do we want to keep up with them? Do we want to share our lives and what is going on? Or did we simply hit "accept" when the friend request came through and never thought about them again?

Social media is all about connecting. You can connect with incredible humans and never once be in their physical presence. As I looked back, I realized that the shift for me happened when I started to not just see my network online as just random people that I didn't care about and only knew, sort of. But it completely shifted when I started to take my network seriously and started to care about them.

Eight years ago, my cousin (probably out of pity) and three strangers interacted with my post on Facebook. The post said, "The traffic on the White Horse Pike sucks." Riveting, I know! If you read that status, how would you feel? Most of you may not know the road or have any experience or feelings about it. Eight years ago, I was not thinking about my network. I was posting small things that weren't impacting anyone at all. What was the objective of this post? What was I hoping to accomplish with it? These are the questions that most people don't ask when they go to post on Facebook or social media.

Your network matters and is essential to building your business. It doesn't matter if they buy from you or become a team member in your business, but you want to think about who you are posting to and why it matters to them. Here are a couple of questions that can help you get more clear about your posts and using social media in a serving way. "Who am I? What are my values? How can I help and serve? How can I make someone feel valid and connected from thousands of miles away? How could I form a relationship so they could feel my truth and intention? What is interesting to me that I can share that will be interesting to them? What solutions am I offering?"

My cousin probably didn't care about the traffic. It was insignificant with no education, call to action or even a funny story. The post was bland and fell flat. If I were to go back and think about my network, I would have created a completely different post. As you build a foundation on social media, start by thinking about your network and how you want to show up for them. When I went from venting to value, my posts started changing, and I got way more interaction than I did before.

Coach's Notes: Social media is called social media for a reason. Be social. The network marketers who have the most success on social media have learned how to use it the right way. Brenda summed up best when she said, "Social media is all about connecting. You can connect with incredible humans and never once be in their physical presence. As I looked back, I realized that the shift for me happened when I started to not just see my network online as just random people that I didn't care about and only knew, sort of. But it completely shifted when I started to take my network seriously and started to care about them."

Many call it fake chit-chat. I look at it completely differently. Yes, you need to guard your time but think of it this way. Just be a good human being. Become a networker first and a network marketer second. Once I discovered how to be a networker first, the doors of success opened for me.

Personal Development

The second place I saw change on my timeline was when I started to take personal development seriously. Listen, I get it; you probably have been told time and time again, but I'm here to tell you that change starts when you start to change internally. I didn't understand the 1% compound rule, but I knew that if I showed up a little better and made people feel a little better, more people would connect with me. I was becoming a product of the law of attraction without realizing it. So ask yourself right now, "What am I doing to change myself internally? How dedicated am I to personal development and doing the work I need to do?"

I started to dig deeper into my own personal development and really started to figure out who I was. The personal development dots started to connect, and I started to create some external changes that aligned with the internal changes I had been working on. Personal development can feel daunting, and I know many people get hung up on where to begin. Let me give you the first step. Start by finishing this book! Then go right out and get *The Game of Networking* by Rob Sperry. These two books are great starting points to your own personal development journey with a paycheck! (If you take it seriously and take action.)

Embody

The third thing I saw that changed over my social media timeline was something I call embodiment. It wasn't until I started walking beside and becoming a true representation of my products that I felt completely aligned with my audience. I couldn't serve my audience when I wasn't using my own products. I couldn't serve my audience if I was using my products and loving them, and not sharing!

When I allowed myself to fall madly in love with the process and actually share about it, I saw myself slowly entering a new playing field. My network watched my life change right before their eyes because I was willing to let them come along and post about it. As I started to embody the change, I noticed that consistency with posting became simple because my daily activities aligned with my mission. I allowed myself a complete lifestyle change to happen. I publicly documented it and brought my network along with me. They didn't have to question if the products worked or if the opportunity provided me with the income; my journey told the story and became all the social proof I needed. My life was in alignment with my opportunity.

The goal was never to lose myself in my brand but to have it become an extension of me. The more I shared, the more my audience flourished, and people became more engaged. My audience was witnessing my growth, and I was showing them how they could do it too. I showed them it was possible and as they watched the blueprint come into fruition. It became just as natural for me to share my opportunity and products as it was to share my children's achievements. Consistency, transparency, and integrations are the formula to success on social media.

Your Next Steps

So what are your next steps? First, I want you to do your own investigation on your personal timeline. What do you post about? How are you showing up on social media? Cultivating connection is key. In order to do that, we want to first know how you are doing. It's not a problem if you find yourself lacking in this department. That's why you are here!

Once you have taken a look at your own timeline, decide what you want to change in order to create value and connection with your network. It can be a commitment to one or two simple steps. You can share more tips, stop complaining so much, or even start commenting back when someone leaves you a comment. Pick a couple of things and stick with them.

Next, I want you to think about how you are responding, reacting, and interacting with your audience on their timelines and DMs (direct messages). Most people tend to miss out on some of the most important aspects of social media. The connection! I once listened to training, and he said that the crucial times to connect with people are in moments of celebration and sorrow. I had never connected the importance when it came to building a solid connection, but people are posting celebrations and sorrows on social media because they are seeking connection from their network.

I'll give you an example. If a beloved pet has been lost, there are usually hundreds of people that express their condolences in the comment section. But how many people actually take the initiative to give that grieving friend time and validation of their loss in the DMs, or even better, in person. Connection means that we are taking the next step. We are sending a private message, creating a voice clip, or picking up the phone and giving them a call. Lasting impact is created during these times because people are asking for connection, and it will be remembered.

The last step that I want to share with you is simple but it can be the most challenging when starting a business. Be human. You can connect with people in genuine ways while sharing your opportunity or product. Remember that everyone is struggling with something and that everyone is craving connection. Lock eyes with people, take a step above the minimum when you are interacting online, and always think about how you can support other people through your posts. You can truly make a lasting impact on someone and never meet them in person!

Coach's Notes: Your social media is your brand. Do not overcomplicate it but make sure you pay attention to it. Be deliberate on the consistent themes you talk about. Who are you? How can you help others get to know you better in an authentic way? I still say the greatest compliment I receive pertaining to social media is when I first meet someone in person, and they tell me that they already feel like they know me. That's the power of social media done right!

"If there's a will, there's a way!
If there's no will, I am a way!!!
— Angela Merkel

CHRISTIAAN J. PETERS

- "Documentation beats conversation."
- 15+ Years in the industry and was active in five different companies.
- Always reached one of the highest ranks in each company and participated in the international leadership.
- Brought three concepts from the USA to Europe & one from Europe to USA and Asia.
- Build multiple 10,000+ organizations.
- Is working on all continents in more than 40+ countries.

How to recruit 75% more people if you just don't talk about your product or service!

(The basic psychology to make it in this industry.)

I've learned from my mentors that the difference between the successful and unsuccessful in our industry is that the successful people do the "BASICs" better.

I want to teach you one of the most important basics I have learned in this chapter. In my case, only after I was four or five years into this business. So I hope it gives you a shortcut to your success, and it will open your eyes to what it is that we actually do in Network Marketing.

What I see on a daily basis is that people outside our industry but also people in our industry think that what we do is "selling a product or service." Where this comes from is obvious because this is how we have framed our whole life. However, the big question is, "Is this true or not ?"

Let me tell you that I have been in this industry for 15+ years now, and I have been responsible for close to 100 million in volume. I have never sold and will never sell one product or service in my life.

WHY?

If you like to sell, do so, but Network Marketing is about "DUPLICATION", and I know that most people can`t sell, don`t like to sell, and suck at it. Therefore if selling is what we do, the duplication is difficult. This is one of the significant issues in our industry why we are not bigger and grow faster as we do. We, the people in the industry, don`t even know or are clear on what it is that we do! Because I don`t have to and I don`t like selling. So what is the solution?

To me, what we do is "find a problem and solve that problem for a price." So that means first we have to find "the problem" with the person we prospect. Here already, most people error because they pitch that person immediately with how good their product or service is, etc., etc., blah, blah, blah.

Coach's Notes: It has been fun to watch Christiaan's success and implement exactly what he has taught you. What really stood out to me is his association with what selling is. There are so many different varying opinions

in network marketing about selling. Christiaan has created a powerful GIVERS mentality. He has created an association of simply finding a problem and GIVING people a solution. I see so many network marketers trying to convince others to buy their products rather than stopping to ask good quality questions to see what their needs really are. Once you learn those you don't FEEL like you are selling but instead, you feel like you are simply HELPING.

I believe that just like a doctor, you should first analyze with your prospect what the problem is, and more often than not, it is not directly what your "product or service" can solve, but your "business opportunity" can. I will show you directly what I mean. A doctor is also not directly going to cut you open when you come into his office, right? No, he asks you direct questions, and based on his expertise, he will send you either to the hospital to get surgery or home to take some rest. Shouldn`t we do something similar? Wouldn`t that make sense?

Suppose you learn to ask the right questions (remember, the one who asks questions is in charge of the conversation)! So if your prospect starts asking you all kinds of questions, guess what happened? Yes, you lost control over the conversation, and you never want to have that)! I can`t go into the details on what questions exactly in this chapter because that in itself could be a chapter. What I can say is that you should start the conversation with questions like you have no Network Marketing opportunity or product or service. Talk like you would if you met that person in any other normal situation outside of Network Marketing.

There is a good reason why we have two ears and one mouth. We should listen more than we talk. In the combination of asking questions and listening to understand the answers, your prospect will give you all the information you need to figure out the problem.

Wouldn't it make sense that if the person himself told you what the problem is and you offered him a solution for that problem, this person would be more likely to listen to you on how you can solve his problem? I sure do hope that we can agree on this!

In my 15+ years of experience talking to more than 40,000 people I found out that there are many problems people can have, but you can narrow it down to 4 major issues. Let me state them all 4 for you.

1. People are looking for more "**MONEY**."

Most likely, this is not something people will immediately admit, but again if you ask the right questions, look at where they live, how they dress, and how they generate income, you can get a pretty good idea. It may not always be 100% correct, but usually, you are not far off either.

2. People are looking for more "**TIME**."

Believe it or not but there are people that genuinely have enough money. But what usually also is the case in that scenario is that those people are very busy generating that money. Working eighty or ninty hours a week or more is no exception for them, leaving little time for family, friends, and hobbies.

3. People seek more "**RECOGNITION**."

The number one reason most people leave a job is not the money. It is the lack of recognition by their superiors for the work and effort they do. You pay people like shit (and mostly this is the case), but if you make them feel appreciated, they will crawl for you and go above and beyond to get the job done.

4. Some issues related to **"HEALTH."**

I never knew that a human being could have so many issues with health, as I saw and learned in the last fifteen years. I think we all know that it is next to impossible to find a person with no health issue whatsoever.

OK, now here comes (hopefully) the BIGGGGG eye-opener and lesson for you!

If you talk to a prospect, as I tried to teach you, and you find out that the main problem with that person is **"MONEY."**

What will provide that person more money?

A) Your product or service or B) Your business opportunity

I hope that we all can agree that it will be B) **Your business opportunity**

If you talk to a prospect, as I tried to teach you, and you find out that the main problem with that person is **"TIME."**

What will provide that person more time?

A) Your product or service or B) Your business opportunity

I hope that we all can agree that it will be **B) Your business opportunity**

If you talk to a prospect, as I tried to teach you, and you find out that the main problem with that person is **"RECOGNITION."**

What will provide that person more recognition?

A) Your product or service or B) Your business opportunity

I hope that we all can agree that it will be **B) Your business opportunity**

If you talk to a prospect, as I tried to teach you, and you find out that the main problem with that person is something with **"HEALTH"** (assuming that you are in a health-related opportunity, if not, the principle most likely still works or maybe needs to be framed a bit different, but you will understand)

What will support that person in his health?

A) Your product or service or B) Your business opportunity

I hope that we all can agree that it will be **A) Your product or service**

Coach's Notes: Human nature is very predictable. Christiaan has identified the main reasons why most people are interested. He has given you what most prospects are thinking. This gives you a huge head start in finding what their problem is and their true desires are. He gave the Dr. example earlier of you finding the problem and prescribing the solution. Now he just gave you more steps on exactly how one can do that. You can see why he has had so much success.

So if we are still on the same page together, you have learned and seen that most likely, in seventy five percent of the cases, it would be more beneficial to offer and show your prospect your business opportunity first and tell him how this would help; solve his "problem." Suppose you become good at this (and yes, it might take some practice, so take it to more people, not less). In that case, it doesn't matter what product or service you work with because the prospect has already accepted the fact that your business opportunity helps him solve his problem, and the product or service is collateral.

Please do not understand me wrong that a product or service is not important; it is very important. But if you just focus on that, you miss out on 75% of your potential, and as a business owner/entrepreneur, wouldn`t that be a shame?

I want you to think of this.....

If the people fifteen years ago came to me and talked about their amazing products, I probably would have kicked them out of my office because I had no interest or relationship with them. But thank God they came and talked to me about my situation. As an architect and real estate developer, my problem was time. They offered, through their business opportunity, a solution to my time constraints with their products that I took for granted. If they had chose the path of products and services in the last 15 years, not close to 100 million in product volume would have went to the marketplace. Think about how much money people (including me) earned on that!

Last but not least.....Nobody owns a drill machine because it was their lifelong dream to own a drill machine. No, they bought a one-time one because it could solve a problem they had, being they needed holes in their wall. It is as simple as that, and the person who sold them the drill machine did not say, "oh, look what a nice color it has," "look how many rpm it has," etc. No, the focus on the problem do you have a concrete wall or a wooden wall, then you need this drill machine. Period!

This is the gain in our industry. Around ninty eight percent of the people in it just talk about their product, product, product. Primarily because they were introduced based on the product, fell in love with their product, and were trained on the product later on. Like I said, there is basically nothing wrong with that, it`s just that you miss out on so much potential that other people like me love to take. Don`t give them the opportunity!

In closing, I want to give you some more ideas to talk about when it comes to business and generic opportunities for anybody.

- Think about the value of **"RESIDUAL INCOME,"** and explain to people what it can mean for them!

    Having this type of "recurring income" allows you (if you have built something significant, of course) to take time off in bad situations, for example, if a family member is sick or dying. Or when you've lost your job, still income is coming in even though you might be temporarily inactive for a few weeks or months.

- The opportunity to create a **"LEGACY INCOME"** and explain to people how that works!

    Let's hope not, but we cannot exclude it either too; you die....that doesn't mean that the people in your team die or stop working, so that means that you can transfer the income to your spouse, children, or even grandchildren if you like. What is the value of this opportunity alone?

- The opportunity to create your own **"RETIREMENT,"** explain to people how that works!

    You don't need to die! If you build something of significance, you can take a step back if you taught your organization well and run by itself without you. The income will still be there.

I hope this chapter brought you value and possibly opened your eyes. It changed my career forever for the better and skyrocketed it to where I am right now. I hope this knowledge will bring good to you too.

Sincerely yours,

Christiaan J. Peters
Entrepreneur & Network Marketing Professional

Coach's Notes: As I always say, "good leaders have vision whereas great leaders give vision." Christiaan gives that clear vision at the end. He knows that for every opportunity to have a conversation with a prospect whether it be a quick voice message, zoom or a phone call you are always finding ways to cast YOUR VISION. You want people to see themselves doing the business. You want to empower others. One statement that massively stood out to me was, "explain to people what it can mean for them!"

"Success is the sum of small efforts-repeated day in and day out."

-Robert Collier

"Desire is the key to motivation, but it's determination and commitment to an unrelenting pursuit to your goal-a commitment to excellence-that will enable you to attain the success you seek."

-Mario Andretti

DEBRAISHA TONEY-HALE

- Top one percent in my company for the past five years while being a six-figure earner.

- Hit several top ranks like Platinum and Crown Club 25.

- Team of more than 90,000 and growing!

- A recipient of "Leads from the front" award.

- Dedicated to teaching others the way.

YOUR TEN CORE COMMITMENTS TO ACHIEVING THE SUCCESS YOU DESIRE

I know that if you can create ten core commitments from the very beginning of your business, you can create any type of success that you desire. Creating and living these ten core commitments will be your ultimate road map to success. Let`s jump in and learn the top ten core commitments to achieving the success you desire.

Coach's Notes: Debraisha is one of the most ENERGETIC leaders I have ever worked with. She walks into a room, and there is instant energy. Like all leaders, she has had many ups and downs, but she is always constantly pushing herself to be better. She has created ten core commitments, which is an assessment of why she has had so much success and so many others. Remember, as Jim Rohn says, "success leaves clues."

1. YOUR WHY!

Most people have a reason for beginning or starting a company. It could be extra money for a vacation, tax write-off, debt-free life, tired of living paycheck to paycheck, college fund, or living a life they have only dreamed of while sleeping.

YOUR WHY should be three things: Personal, Powerful, and Purposeful. When your WHY is personal, it is very dear to you. Sometimes we take on someone else`s, which means nothing to us. When it is personal to you, you move differently. You are determined; you get back up and go back at it, and nothing stops you. My WHY is what I would pull out when I had a hard day and needed that push or the day before went horribly wrong, but yet, I had to show up. It was then that I discovered that my WHY was POWERFUL! When I thought about what it is that I wanted to accomplish through my WHY, it pushed me to keep going. It was my motivation; it was my accountability partner, and it was my everything. It has to make you cry, laugh, persevere, and so much more. Make sure your why has purpose! And I am not talking about those new shoes but something that has substance to it. Imagine what you could do and how much you could save if you paid off all of your debt in a debt-free life. Purpose also gives passion. Allow yourself to feel your why, love your why, commit to your why, but most of all, see it come to pass.

2. KNOWledge is POWER!

You hold the key to your SUCCESS! Take time to learn about your company, your product, the incentives, and the promotions. Knowing your business so that you have a full understanding gives you the opportunity to KNOW what is available to you and how to set your goals to reach the level that you desire. Success to me and success to you can look very different. Take the first step of knowing your why and tie it into your company. This level can bring me to an option of retirement, where this number of sales can cover my household bills. I would also go to the next level of breaking each level down and what is needed to build a team or sales. Most of the time, it can be a numbers game. How many do I need? What is my sales target? Break it down, and know what it takes to accomplish the goal.

3. SET GOALS!

We all need goals. We need a vision! Where are we going? What are your desires? What do you need? What do you want to accomplish? Set goals to put a (POA) plan of action in place. We should have short-term/long-term goals. Your short-term goals should align with your long-term goals. This will help you have a starting point, and at any given time, you can change whatever needs to be changed.

When you think about the CORE commitments, each builds on the other. Your WHY, KNOWing and understanding your business, and now you can put your goals in place. Each commitment matters! Do not overwhelm yourself; your goals will help you to focus on where your energy should be along with your plan of action. I usually have three goals that I start with, and those goals are written down. There are three things that you must do with your goals.

1. Determine your short term/long term goals.

2. Write them down and put them in a location where you can see them daily.

3. Determine a plan of action.

Coach's Notes: When we begin, we just want to make our money back, which is good enough. As the possibility of our dreams and hopes grow, we need to grow. This is when we begin to ask ourselves what we want and why we want it. This is when we start to learn more and increase our knowledge to go to the next level. True knowledge means you are taking action and being clear on your goals. Debraisha is helping you accelerate the learning curve by laying out ten specific steps to success.

4. Daily Method of Operation! (DMO)

We all want to make sure we are utilizing our time and efforts with what will yield the best results. You know your goals; now, what can you implement daily to get to those results? When I first retired from being a professional school counselor in 2018, I was very nervous and kept thinking to myself, what will my day look like? I had been in my career field of education for seventeen years, and now, it was time to take the leap—the leap into being a total entrepreneur. I had prayed and fasted, my husband was very supportive, and a few months before that, we had hit a major rank. If I had been utilizing a DMO, it might have eased my nerves a little because I had a view of my day or outlook on this entrepreneur stance.

My daily method starts with prayer first, even though I am the first one in my household. What is vital for you and needs to be done should be placed in your DMO. Do you have team zooms, or LIVES, exercise, meditation, time to organize, homework with the kids, and so much more to get done in your day? This is a great way to build your day to be able to use your time responsibly and to make sure that your income-producing activities are getting done as often as you need them to reach those goals. (IPA`s)

5. Personal Development!

I LOVE to LEARN! Take time to grow. We have many opportunities to learn, and so many things are at our fingertips. There is nothing like attending a Breakthrough Mastermind with Rob Sperry. I must admit, being in person and feeling the energy is amazing. However, we also have zooms, podcasts, training, personal development, books to read, and social media. We think about those conversations that we have with our uplines, other network marketers, or those who have accomplished a goal that we are working towards. We should always be in a position to grow and learn. We are just like the title of Michelle Obama`s book, *BECOMING*! We are becoming our best selves, and personal development helps us reach that point. Keep an open mindset and give others a chance. I feel as if I can learn something from everybody. Even those who are in a different position, we all have a story, a journey. Find time for yourself to educate yourself.

6. Unpack your BAG

Life has a way of attaching things to us that are not always easy to get rid of: the things that hold you back. Think about things that may have affected you in moving forward. It could be a good friend or a family member who doesn`t support your business. They may be a negative Nancy, always bringing negative vibes to you about your business. Well, unpack that person, love them but do not talk about your business with them. Do not let them hold you back from GREATNESS. You may have low self-esteem, it could be fear, laziness, procrastination, or a number of things, but it has to go. UNpack it, get rid of it, tell it bye-bye.

Take time, to be honest with yourself; what is holding you back from your next level? What has attached itself to you, and has it slowed you down? We all have something to overcome but do not wait too long. It has taken enough from you. Clean out those bags. It is time for you to breathe again. Take a piece of paper, write down that one thing or even if it is more than one thing, look at it, and then tear it up and throw it away. This is a new season for you, and it is time to let go!

7. Take the Limits off!!

I must be honest; there was a long time before I realized I was living in a limited mindset. As an educator, we always had a pay scale. A pay scale showed us how much we could make with a certain degree and our years of experience. I could pretty much tell you what I would make in twenty years, twenty five years, etc. I was paid once a month, and it was a set salary. When I started network marketing, their pay scale had potential. Wait, I can make how much, in a month, in a year. I can get paid every day for my product!!! Music to my ears. It was then that I realized there is so much out there for my family and me, and I have to remove the limits of how much money we can make. In 2018, I became a six-figure earner and had every year since then, but I had to remove the limited mindset. You may have a different scenario but take the limits off so you can soar. Our mindset matters. What has been taught to us or even what we have been exposed to may positively or negatively impact us and our mindset? Think about it real hard; what has kept you in a box from your full potential?

8. Have a Spirit of URGENCY!!

"Without a sense of urgency, desire loses its value," Jim Rohn. Take advantage of the NOW! Get up and go right now. Tomorrow isn`t promised, and next year may look very different for you, your family, your team, and your strongest leg. Why put off things that you can do today for tomorrow. I have learned that every business has a season of seedtime and harvest. You don't want to miss your season, it may come back again, but if you move now, it can happen now. Do not take for granted the time we have now; instead, move with it as if there is no tomorrow. Every day creates another opportunity for us to make moves in the right direction, move and move now! I often shared with others to have a right now spirit, but they didn't move. It wasn't urgent for them, and because of that, they are still where they were and never got to that desired level of success they wished to have.

Coach's Notes: Urgency is synonymous with wealth. Too many network marketers claim to have so much vision but are their actions matching that vision? Is your action matching your vision? I am not speaking to you about the number of total hours you are working. I am speaking to you about your FOCUS. Ask yourself this question to help you focus and create urgency. Is what I am doing right now making me the most amount of money?

9. Set Your Atmosphere Every Day!

Entrepreneurship can have its moments. Most of us have worked and are still working very hard to win or begin a new chapter. You have to OWN your day by setting the atmosphere. Decree it and declare it! I use daily affirmations, and they have been very powerful in my life. I stop and say it out loud. I am a winner. I am confident. I am an overcomer! Today is going to be awesome! Speak life! Create your own atmosphere of who you are or what you are becoming. Do not be scared to open your mouth and speak. Say it loud, say it proud and say it with confidence. Let nothing and no one hold you back from speaking life over your business and where you are going. Your desired level of Success will need to live in an atmosphere of belief and positivity. You have the power and the ability to create a winning atmosphere even when that day wasn't the best. Set your atmosphere every day!

10. IT's YOURS; go for it!

Believe that you can achieve! Go for it! Everything your heart desires to have in your business, in your life, you can have it. Put your best foot forward and GO. You may get knocked down, but get back up and keep running. The sky is the limit, and there are people who believe in you, but you believe in yourself most of all! Spread your wings and FLY!!

DEBRAISHA TONEY-HALE

"Don't treat them the way they are; treat them the want you want them to be."

—Tom Dorance

HEATHER BAUMAN

- Joined network marketing on Jan 5, 2020.

- #2 team in two separate companies, by helping bring 9 million in total team sales while training, marketing professional barrel horses, running a successful equine boarding facility, and representing cutting edge Brazilian lightweight seven saddles, South Dakota made Sammy`s Flaxseed Oil, and a unique feed by Chaffhaye LLC.

- Six-figure earner in the first year of MLM.

- Consistently sold up to six-figures in horse sales nationwide for the past seven years.

The first time I heard this quote, I wasn`t sure if he was talking about people or horses. I later realized that he was talking about both. I have spent countless hours around horses, and they have taught me more about life than anything else. I have learned about relationships, people, overcoming fear, and even the impact of how I was showing up in my business. Horses even taught me how to set myself up for success and get big wins in life and business.

I wish everyone had the ability to get on a horse and learn what I have, but lucky for you, I have taken everything I have learned and put it right here in this chapter. I will teach you some of the best practices for ultimate success. These can be used and applied anytime or anywhere.

Coach's Notes: One of the greatest aspects of network marketing is the person you become. Heather teaches you how to be a good human being! When I first heard my mentor talk about that concept, I remember rolling my eyes. I thought, "of course, you can say that because you make millions of dollars!" The more money I made, the more I realized that statement was true. As I learned to become a better version of myself, I started to have more success in all aspects of life, including my network marketing business.

Practice ONE-Come from a place of EMPATHY

Putting yourself in others shoes gives you a perspective of others and their needs, desires, and situations. We are not all the same. We think, feel, act, and react differently based on our experiences. If we only come from our viewpoint, we miss the opportunity to connect with people. You can only draw a small percentage of people that think like you if you can`t have an empathetic view. This will limit your potential and growth if you stay closed off to other people`s perspectives.

Since horses can`t talk, I had to learn to communicate through energy, timing, feeling, and coming from a place of compassion and empathy. It`s no different with people. It`s a lot easier to feel the direction best suited for someone when you know what they are saying and where they are coming from. Be emphatic and look for the place you can help fill a need for the person you are talking to. Listen first before saying anything.

Practice TWO-Have a servant's heart

When you can focus on serving others, you will find yourself growing in the capacity to make a HUGE impact in other people`s lives. You have to shift out of thinking of yourself and shift into a servant`s heart to make a big difference. The ripple effect is very real. It`s incredible how much reach you can acquire through helping one person. Plant seeds daily through service and continues to take care of that seed. You will eventually reap the benefits of the harvest. When farmers plant a seed, they don`t dig it up every day to see how it`s growing. They continue to water and care for it with the belief that their efforts will pay off and they will reap the benefits.

Relationships with people are the same. When you genuinely care about others, invest in the relationship, and pour into it, both you and the other person will reap the benefits from that relationship. When you can serve others knowing that you may get absolutely nothing in return, that is when you put yourself in the greatest position to influence others.

I am a natural giver, and I have seen play out in my lifetime and again that what goes around comes around. The universe recognizes your servant`s heart and giving nature, and it will return to you in abundance. This starts with your habits and mindset. Be an authentic server and giver with your daily actions.

Practice THREE-The one percent rule

I believe in attaining one percent better every day. A very respected horse clinician that I`ve had the honor of riding with came up with this rock-solid concept. He uses it in many areas and teaches others how to apply it in their riding and daily habits. We sometimes get overwhelmed with the process and the steps that it takes to get to the results that we all so desperately want. It can even feel hard to get started when you think about everything you have to do. When I am onboarding new information for myself and seeing everything that I need to get done, I start looking for the one percent. I am looking to see the one thing I can do to improve or get started today.

It's pretty amazing how it takes the weight off my shoulders knowing that I just need to get one percent improvement that day. I have also found, that this helps flow happen and things seem to run so much smoother. If you can break your big tasks down into the smaller one percent, you will see how consistent you can be. Over one hundred days you will find that you have created simple systems that you are consistently doing and it will have you operating at one hundred percent. Keeping it simple can be taught effectively to others, which creates duplication. It's human nature to want to control the outcome.

Coach's Notes: Sometimes we walk, sometimes we jog, sometimes we sprint but as long as we are always focused on a little bit of progress it makes all of the difference. Often, network marketers compare their chapter 3 to someone else's chapter 22. We get way too high when we have success and way too low emotionally when we have a bad day, week, or month. By focusing on the one percent rule you narrow your focus on PROGRESS. Tony Robbins says his definition of happiness is progress.

Practice FOUR-Leave your ego at the door

One of my favorite quotes is from Maya Angelou, "People will forget what you said, people will forget what you did, but people will not forget how you made them feel." Every time I step into the arena with my horse or the arena of life, I leave my ego at the door. Horses will humble you to the very core. They don't care who you are, or who you think you are. If you can't find humor in tough situations, it will be hard to make it far. You have to keep things light and positive and end on a good note.

I had not truly understood my potential for a very long time. We all have limiting beliefs. I have had a lot of them! Once I came upon an opportunity to manage a brand new horse boarding facility. Fear immediately took a hold of me. I had to set small attainable goals so that I wouldn't focus on the fear. Every day I checked off one accomplishment. Soon those started to add up and I started to see myself as growing and successful. But I had to leave my ego at the door and allow myself to be a beginner.

Occasionally I see people let their egos get in the way of their business. They start to act differently and sometimes even start to lie to themselves and others. Integrity is everything. It's what you do and how you are when no one else is looking. Integrity and ego can't exist together. It is either one or the other. When I say check your ego at the door, that also means to fully embody integrity. When you speak, others will recognize it as your truth or your ego speaking. No matter the situation, make the right choice. Checking our ego at the door also helps us show loyalty and respect to others, even when we don't see eye to eye. When you can consistently show up in who you are, others will find trust there. People follow and invest in others that have integrity. Trust and honesty are priceless, and solid relationships are built on this and will stand the test of time.

Practice FIVE-Find strength in the individual

It's easy to get stuck in a negative spin on life or your business. Don't do it! You choose what you focus on. If you can focus on the strengths of others, it will help build confidence in them. When you focus on the weakness of others it tends to catch up to them and you. Focus on the strengths and watch how that will organically become an asset to you and them.

There is no need to be the master of everything. It's ok to lean on others. That is what makes up a team. This is also where finding strengths in others becomes an asset to you and them. You all don't need to be experts. You can collectively come together and create something amazing by utilizing everyone's strengths. A team creates success as a whole. A team creates a force that no one person can do alone.

I have always been a competitive person. I had to learn the value of teamwork. I found that I would never have truly lasting success without the leverage of other people on the team, seeing and honoring their strengths. You have to be willing to lock arms with others and create a strong community. It will lift you all higher, and believe me, there is plenty to go around! Every single person is unique and can bring something of value. Other people's success will never hinder yours.

I was raised to believe you are only as good as your team, your employees, or in my case, my equine team consisting of me, my horse, trainers, facility, etc. This helped me surround myself with people who were willing to dedicate their lives to being the best at what they did. Let people on your team become the best. Support them.

Practice SIX-Never fear failure

Your best teacher is learning to fail. I truly tried everything wrong to figure out what worked for me. One of the most valuable lessons I learned is to always treat people with care. How you leave them feeling really can create an entire impression. In this business, there are a lot of failures. See these as learning opportunities. When you see your team fail, think about how you want to be treated through failure and adversity. In your own business, you will talk to a lot of people. Be thoughtful even if the conversation doesn`t go the way you thought it would. Don`t take rejection as a personal attack. It is more about the other person than it is about you most of the time. Stay kind, and use the rejection or failure to learn and grow.

When I never fear failure, I also can continue to learn, be a student, and make mistakes. You are your greatest asset. Knowledge is power, but never "know too much." Always remain the student. Some of the most beneficial lessons came out of nowhere and from unexpected people. When I remind myself that I am always a student, I am more open to learning from different people and experiences. Always invest in yourself and your growth.

Practice SEVEN-Bet on yourself

You can`t let fear control your life. Everything that I wanted was on the other side of fear. It was scary to bet on myself, but I am so grateful I did. I had so many times that I could have said that I was done or that what I wanted was too big.

I had to face my fear of climbing on the back of a larger-than-life colt. I had to face my fear of traveling across the country with my dog and a trailer full of horses all by myself. I had to face my fear of entering the richest races in the country. I also had to face my fear of speaking in public, which was incredibly hard for me. At every single moment, I had a chance to quit. But I didn`t. I bet on myself.

Betting on yourself takes a risk. I wasn`t winning all of the time. But I always say, If I`m not winning, I am learning. It`s ok to adjust and adapt your plans, but make sure you do it for the right reasons. Sometimes we get blown around a bit, and most of the time works out for the better. Be open to this. Be teachable, and always bet on yourself.

Network marketing found me by chance. I was in a spot in my life where I was open, and it felt right. Initially, I had no idea what the opportunity would do for me. But I followed these practices and kept consistent. I truly believe that I could accomplish this. Anyone who puts their mind to it can, too—a small-town horse-crazy girl who never really took a no at face value.

Horses sure taught me a lot, but very little of it had to do with horses....

Coach's Notes: Bet on yourself. God didn't send you to this earth to be average! If someone else can do it, you can do it. It may take you longer but so what. It is possible. Begin to look for evidence to justify every reason WHY you will be successful. Begin to train your brain to look for solutions rather than problems. As you shift to this type of growth mindset, it is no longer a question of if you will have success but when you will have it.

HEATHER BAUMAN

"Think like a queen. A queen is not afraid to fail. Failure is another stepping stone to greatness."

— Oprah Winfrey

JENNIFER PIPER KENNEDY

- First and only Canadian in her company to reach Top Elite Black level.

- Speaker for Most Powerful Women in Network Marketing and Go Pro.

- Created systems that produced a 30:1 customer/marketer ratio on her team

- Seven-figure earner.

- Advisory board for the company.

Building a business with stories

Storytelling is... an art.

Storytelling is described as an art... the "art" of storytelling. Like art, it requires creativity, skill, practice, practice, and more practice.

Your story is your superpower. It took me a while to understand this concept, and I would shy away from parts of my story. But, once I realized my story was my superpower, there was no holding me back.

My entrepreneurial journey started as a kinesiologist who fell into becoming a business owner. I owned three different traditional storefront businesses back in 2007, a grocery store, a clothing store, and a Sears appliance store. I loved working with people. I loved marketing and everything that went along with owning a business. But brick-and-mortar businesses aren't the best business models for women who are moms.

When I started to have kids, I felt this enormous sense of never being able to do anything successfully. For any of you moms, you probably know how this feels. In less than five years, I had three boys, and my priorities completely shifted. I still loved being an entrepreneur, but I was working the business six or seven days a week, and I was continually falling short and had zero free time.

I realized that I didn't have any quality time with my kids. The older they got, the more I found myself missing the moments that mattered the most. It didn't feel great to come home exhausted and not be fully present. I was starting to have '*mom guilt*' because I realized that the daycare was raising my kids. The women at daycare were seeing my kids' first steps. They were having those "firsts" that I would never experience.

I finally reached my breaking point one morning while getting my kids ready for daycare. They were little at the time, and I had asked my older boys to start to get their shoes on while I helped my youngest. As little boys do, the boys were messing around and were slow to get their shoes on. I yelled at them to get their shoes on in a panic to open the store on time.

When they didn't do it, I picked them up, put them in the car, and got them to daycare as fast as I could. I ended up at the store and completely melted down.

This was not the mom I wanted to be.

This was not the person I wanted to be.

I had massive *mom guilt* set in, but I couldn't see a way out of it.

Another thing that was happening was that I was struggling with money management. The idea of owning businesses is amazing and exciting. But, in actuality, there are a lot of unknowns and fears that go with owning a traditional brick-and-mortar business. Maybe some of you can relate.

For example, I would do the books and find that all the money was tied up in inventory, staffing costs, or overhead. So, as successful as I looked at owning these businesses, there wasn't a lot of extra money, time, or freedom.

I was stuck in the struggle. I loved owning the businesses, and I loved being an entrepreneur and all of that that came along with it, but I was having a lot of guilt with the kids and no time and money. So that moment for me was when I started to think, "okay, maybe there's something else." So I decided to call my girlfriend Kristine, who was involved in a direct sales company. She had approached me for a year about looking into her business.

I had always looked down on it as something that bored housewives did. But after that terrible morning with my kids and my desire for more quality time with them, I called Kristine. It was 10 a.m. on a weekday, and she answered the phone from her balcony. She and her husband were having coffee in their bathrobes.

At 10 a.m. on a weekday!

At that moment, I realized there was a different way to be an entrepreneur, and I was all in for learning how to do it. I booked a party with her, which ended up being the most successful party she had ever had to date. While she was en route to host my party, I knew I was all in and told her I wanted to start the business, and she almost drove off the road! Six months later, I was able to hire a manager for my stores and go all in myself in my new direct sales business.

I can't tell you what a blessing in disguise was for my boys and me. Two years after I started my business, I went through a painful divorce. Not only did that business serve me financially without any child support, but it also got me through with the support of a fantastic network of people.

This industry has changed my life. My only regret is that I didn't believe bigger, earlier. I have a new dream home, my children have been able to travel to places around the world, and I have been able to purchase a beautiful spot on a lake that we used to camp at that now, I will be able to take our grandchildren to and have as a legacy for our future. My team has grown worldwide and financially; this has changed our lives. Since I started this business, I haven't missed one sporting event or activity that my kids have been involved in. I am all in for early morning hockey, baseball tournaments, and volunteering for the events!

I'm hoping that by sharing my story to start this out, you saw something in my story that maybe is like your story, right? One of the most important things you can do as an online entrepreneur is to build your own business that will harness the power of your story. Telling a story is like painting a picture with words. You want people to feel the feelings, see what you see, and hear what you hear.

Stories are important to share for several reasons. First, stories create a connection with your audience. Stories help you become more relatable; they allow people to connect with the message you are sharing and help them connect to you. I have had several people come up to me when we meet, and they say something like, *"I feel like I know you already!"* This happens because of my stories on social media and my willingness to share my struggle and stories.

Second, stories are important because they help you stand out from everyone else. Anyone can sell a product. What sets you apart is your personal experience and the words you use to describe the product, what you like about it, and what it has done for you. Stories build rapport and help create relationships. Stories inspire and motivate. I used to hide that I was a single mom and how I struggled. Then I realized that all of that was my superpower and nothing to hide!

Coach's Notes: Discovering how to tell better stories never ends! The best movies in the world tell the best stories, and we love them. Those who can tell better stories are more entertaining, likable and are better at sales. We aren't talking about telling exaggerated stories but instead learning how to communicate better. If you want to make more money and create that time freedom, focus on Jennifer's tips for telling better stories.

Building Your Story

You have heard the saying, *"facts, tell, stories sell."* When we sell a product, we often talk about all the facts people don't relate to. We miss the entire sale of sharing stories. So learning how to craft a story to create a connection is part of learning how to get the sale. I want to share with you how to craft a compelling story. If you wait until your story is perfect, it will never happen. You have to be willing to share your story before it feels comfortable. You will screw up, and that's okay. Done is better than perfect, and you will get better at it the more you share it. Share your story as often as possible with a variety of people. The more you share, the more you will tweak and improve upon what you are saying. Great stories are simple to tell and simple to remember.

There are three parts to any great story-the before, the pivot and the after.

The BEFORE is the first part of crafting your story. What was your life like before using the product or being in this industry? What is your background? What are your pain points?

My example at the beginning of the chapter was my "before." I had no time, not much extra money, and a ton of mom guilt. That was my BEFORE.

Paint the picture so that people should be able to almost put themselves in the room with you. Take us to that place where we can feel the feelings, see what you see, hear what you hear. Your audience will become emotionally connected to you if you can do that.

So think about your BEFORE. What have you been doing as a profession? What is your family situation? Where have you been struggling? Write down your BEFORE story and how it would help to connect you to others. Think about who you are talking to and how your story will attract your audience to you. We all have pain points in our lives. Things that cause stress and make us stay up at night. It is time, money, work, and relationships for most people.

The PIVOT is the second part of crafting your story

The PIVOT is where your story changes. Every great story has conflict, and the PIVOT is the solution that you found to one or several of your pain points. During this part of your story, you want to share how the solution helped your life. It could be the product, business opportunity, or both. When you think about your PIVOT, you aren't downplaying it as not a big deal. People can relate to your pains and stress. They are looking for solutions too, so make sure to talk about it.

In my story, part of the PIVOT was hearing Kristine tell me she was sitting on her deck having coffee after I had that problematic morning with my boys. I knew she was a successful entrepreneur, but it was a different lifestyle than I was used to. I hadn't ever seen anyone having success in this industry. I realized there was a different way to do business. I share this part of my story because I know there are people out there doing their jobs and feeling like it is the only way to earn money and provide for their families. I share my PIVOT point because I know that other people need to hear the different options so they can have that exact moment I did. Share your PIVOT and make sure you don't downplay how important it was to you and how it changed your life.

The last part of building your story is the AFTER

Think of it as the happily ever after of your story. What is your life like now? What are the pain points that were solved for you? What has changed in your lifestyle? For example, I shared my dream home and vacations with my kids in my story. I also shared about being able to be at all of my kids' activities. That is my AFTER story.

IF you get the BEFORE right, you have people leaning in as you are describing their life right now. What they don't love about it, and/or what they want to change.

If you get the AFTER right it describes what they want for their future, and they can see it.

Your story will evolve over time. If you had asked me about the AFTER in my story two years ago, I wouldn't have said anything about my dream home because I didn't have that dream then! Your AFTER story doesn't have to be about owning homes and vacations. Your AFTER can be making extra money to pay for sports. Maybe you have been able to have extra money for date night, a holiday, or that car payment. Your AFTER can be being able to find a product that is showing promise to help you out.

Your AFTER will be ever-evolving! Please don't shy away from sharing your AFTER because it doesn't feel big enough. That's not a thing! Your story and where you right now matter to people. You will connect with people that I can't connect with because of where you are at in your story. Build your story, think about the three different parts to create, write it down and continue to craft and work on it.

BONUS to your story, share your vision of the FUTURE

When I started making money in this business, I became very aware of what was possible for my life if I was successful. It was exciting to think about the future, and I couldn't help sharing it with other people to show them that it was possible for them. Think about sharing a little bit of your vision for your future and the bigger picture. People love to see possibilities because it helps them see themselves and dream of what could be. People like to be part of the bigger picture.

Your story is about how you overcame the struggle. Your story is a vehicle to share your message and show people how you overcame what you went through. People want to relate to you and your story, but don't get stuck in the struggle. Your story is about overcoming, not staying stuck.

You want to adjust your story depending on who you are talking to. For example, if you are talking to someone struggling with money, you may want to spend a bit more time talking about the financial hardship you went through. You can constantly adjust your story to highlight the different parts of your story. This means that you will have to think about your story from different angles to meet other prospects.

Once you get your stories crafted, you have to start sharing them! Craft the story, and then share it on social media and in-person to whoever you can. If you want to share on social media, you can use reels, lives, or posts to share your story. I recommend that you do some sort of video because it helps you get better at telling your story; so you can rewatch it, adjust your story, and keep practicing it. Plus people LOVE to hear your voice and connect to you. The more you practice your story, the more it will become easy for you, and you will start to know exactly what to share with the group of people you are in front of.

Coach's Notes: I love the breakdown from Jennifer on telling stories. She simplifies it in a way you can measure your own storytelling. Write down those three steps:

1. **Before**
2. **Pivot**
3. **After**

Start small and know that it is ok to screw up initially. You only become better by actually practicing telling your story in real-life situations.

Stories don't stop with you; become a collector and connector through stories

Stories don`t stop with you.

Become a collector and connector through stories.

Once you have crafted your own story, you want to become a collector of stories. So create your storybook filled with stories and social proof, and use that to connect to more people.

There are three types of stories that are useful for you to collect:

1. Product Stories

Listen to other people's results with the product, write them down and share them. It could be people on your team or your customers that have results using the product. Social proof is compelling, and you being able to share others' wins utilizing a product or in your business will help you connect with more people.

2. Business Stories

Collect different stories of all types of people having success in your company. Different backgrounds, careers, ages, educations, and time in the business. Use these to connect to people with similar experiences.

3. Company Stories

Collect great company stories, wins and successes that you can share.

Let go of being attached to the outcome but learn instead to just connect your prospect through a story to a tool. That tool may be a video, a zoom, a messenger chat, or introducing them to a leader. You can do this with stories more successfully than with facts. The more stories we share, the more different people we can connect to that following exposure. Tell the story, connect to a tool, and keep it simple.

When we first start our business, many of us want to wait for our personal product results to start sharing. What if you simply shared stories of other people having results? Your friends and family may even connect better to the social proof of others. Early in my business, I realized the power of connecting my audience to other people's results instead of waiting on my own. Don't hold your business hostage, waiting for your own product story. Use social proof!

You all have a story to tell. So please take what you have learned in this chapter, go craft your story, and start to share it and build your business through the power of story.

Your story is your superpower!

Coach's Notes: This last paragraph should be a significant ah-ha moment. I hear so many network marketers worry that their story isn't strong enough. BORROW from others! There are so many stories within your team or company that can be used. You are simply a connector to information.

"Fear, inherently, is not meant to limit you. Fear is the brain's way of saying that there is something important for you to overcome."

– Yvan Byeajee

JENNIFER STROMAN

- Founder of Sparkle+Roots and Corporate Sponsor leader.

- Small town Texas girl mom, boy grandma, cat lover, and glitter obsessed.

- Industry veteran for over 22 years where she has made six-figures, and is one of the top leaders of her company and leads a multi-million dollar organization with tens of thousands of women with multiple women achieving six-figures and thousands of women earning a monthly "comma" check.

- Co-Author, book contributor, also featured on the cover of a direct sales magazine, event speaker, and trainer for tens of thousands worldwide.

- It is her personal mission is to help female social sellers shatter barriers and become the superhero God created them to be.

But Did You Die?

Since I can remember, I have been a dancer. My mom had me in tap, jazz, and ballet at a young age. She told me that I would complain about halfway through the season, complaining about not wanting to dance anymore, and she'd have to keep dragging me. When the recital came, I lit up!

Isn't this always how it works? We begin something new, and we are excited. Then the newness wears off, so we begin to doubt our decision and want to quit just before it gets exciting. For most of us, it's fear. Fear of messing up, judgment, or commitment. The subconscious mind wants to keep you safe. It's perfectly content if you never challenge yourself, so we immediately want to recoil when things get tough. It doesn't care if you spend your life in your comfort zone.

I love the "but did you die" scene in *The Hangover Part II*. After Mr. Chow was rescued from a hotel's icebox, the scene took place. Phil apologizes and says, "We're just having a bad day." Chow's response of "but did you die" was not just comical but a reminder that things could always be worse.

I often use this phrase to remind my team that the world isn't going to end by facing your fears. You can keep going, and it will be okay, even if you struggle to get there. Think of a tree. As saplings grow, they withstand weather challenges; their roots grow deeper and stronger as they fight wind and storms. For a tree to thrive, it must face adversity.

My youngest daughter, Nickole, has had a love for trees since she could walk. She is mesmerized by their magnitude, beauty, and strength. Science projects always consisted of something to do with trees. To me, they were just trees, but to her, they were the most beautiful life-form after humans. I still roll my eyes when she wants to stop and see a tree up close, but I came to appreciate and love these majestic ornaments of nature because of her. I love business analogies, and just like a mighty tree, a business needs to be nurtured to grow.

Throughout this chapter, I will connect the familiarity of a tree to your business and guide you on how to push past your fears to find the success you truly desire.

Coach's Notes: Before you dive deep into this chapter on FEAR, I want to point out a few things. I know Jennifer extremely well. I have personally coached her, and she has attended several masterminds. She is a top leader in her company. She is a top industry leader. She still deals with fears, but the difference between her and the unsuccessful is that she has learned to go through those fears over and over again. There is a great quote that says, "new levels, new devils."

1. THE ROOT

The roots of a tree provide structural strength to hold the tree in place and help absorb the nutrients it needs to survive. Without the roots, the tree would not exist, so it makes sense we start at the root of it all. There are three things we need to break down to help you understand WHY you get stuck at the starting line.

Identify your Fears

What exactly is it that you're afraid of? Some common fears include:

- Not knowing enough.
- Failure.
- Not being good enough.

- Judgment.
- The unknown.

You're never going to be totally ready. You can take this one day at a time. You don't need everything planned out or a clear path to success. You'll learn from your mistakes and become better.

The issue is we often use our fears as excuses. For example, the fear of not knowing enough could hold you back. You might think you need to explore and research all facts, statistics, product knowledge, etc., but this is holding you back from taking a step forward. There are plenty of resources and opportunities to learn as you build your business. The truth is, you will likely not know everything at first. Fortunately for you, you will have a mentor, leader, or coach who can help guide you.

It's NOT about You

When attending an event, about eighty five percent of people may notice your existence, but not your appearance. Why? Most people are more worried about their own lives and what people think to spend too much time focusing on you. They are too caught up in their insecurities to pay attention to yours. Focus on helping others and stop worrying about yourself.

What if?

We all have "what if" thoughts. We instinctively play out worst-case scenarios. The subconscious mind tries to keep you safe. Redirecting your thoughts is not easy to do when your mind starts wandering down this path. Instead of letting the fear build-up, break it down.

For example, a waitress goes to each table asking customers if they need a refill. If you tell her no, she doesn't go to the back of the kitchen and cry. She's not in a corner, all embarrassed and scared. What does she do? She goes to the following table and asks if they need a refill. She spends NO time worrying about your no and moves on to help the next customer. After reading this, is someone telling you no really that scary?

I want you to hear my voice asking you, "but did you die?" Let me be clear. No one is going to take away your birthday. No one is going to steal your firstborn. Your what ifs are silly, so flip the script... what`s the best-case scenario? Isn`t it worth the risk?

2. THE TRUNK

The trunk and its branches are the main structure that gives a tree its shape. It is strong and resilient. But have you ever looked at a cut tree trunk? The different layers reveal something much more interesting.

The bark and protector of the tree are the outer two layers, but there are three layers I want to hone in on heartwood, sapwood, and cell layer. I know this chapter is about FEAR, but hang with me on this!

The heartwood is the very center of the trunk. It is the "OG" of the tree. This is who you are at your core. It is your foundation. The sapwood is new wood and measures all of its growth, much like you are aging. But, the cell layer is the most important layer of all. It stimulates new growth, much like self-development, and your actions can stimulate growth in your business. Each layer is important for the tree`s growth and lifespan. When the tree doesn`t grow, it doesn`t live long. The same can be said of your business. If you are not fueling your business with new growth, it cannot survive.

Your fears are blocking your growth! Much like the bark of a tree is there for protection, our subconscious mind tries to protect us. Its job is to keep you comfortable and safe, so when you are afraid, your subconscious mind tries to take the fear away and put you back into your comfort zone.

Prepare Yourself

I know it is not easy to overcome fear. Sometimes it can be crippling, and taking action seems daunting. The most effective way to face your fears is to prepare yourself. If you can rewire your brain, control your breathing, and remember why you are doing this, you can confidently take on the fear monster.

1. Rewire your brain

Your thoughts have power. What you speak, you give life to. Your words become a reality, and your actions directly result from your thinking. Those who have a negative mindset produce negative lives. Those who choose to focus on the positive build positive, prosperous lives. Rewiring your brain is a surefire way to face and overcome your fears with courage.

There are three things you can do to retrain your brain:

1. Create or find mantras and affirmations that build you up and increase self-confidence.

2. Consume self-development daily. Whether you read a book, listen to a podcast or watch a video, make time every single day to fill your cup.

3. Combat the negative. Each time you think of something negative, verbally replace it with something positive.

Want to know the fastest trick to rewire your brain? It's the superhero pose challenge. A golden nugget that will blow your mind! This one is a bonus.

Have you heard of the superhero, power, or wonder woman pose? This pose is an expansive posture where you stand with your feet shoulder-width apart, place your hands in a fist on your hips, stand tall, lift your chin, and look upward. Spending at least two minutes a day in this pose will reduce stress and increase confidence. This high-power pose will reduce stress and increase confidence, but it will help you feel more powerful and perform better. It increases testosterone by twenty percent and decreases cortisol levels by twenty five percent. Higher levels of testosterone lead to increased feelings of confidence. Meanwhile, lower cortisol levels lead to decreased anxiety and an improved ability to deal with stress. Amazing, right? TRY IT NOW!

Coach's Notes: Mindset will eat skills and systems for breakfast. Overcoming your fears isn't focused on ENOUGH. Too often, we skip straight to the skills, but here is the issue. If you can't get out of your own head, it won't matter how much your skills increase. Your fears will prevent you from unlocking those skills. It begins with being willing to fight those fears head-on. I love this training because it is a practical guide to help you DEAL with your fears.

2. Control your breathing

Breathing is so important. When we are anxious, we breathe heavier and with shorter breaths. This instantly causes a negative reaction within our body. The key to preventing or stopping your growing anxiety is to control your breathing as soon as possible.

It's amazing how our bodies can calm themselves with a simple breathing technique. When you feel a growing sense of anxiety or fear, take a step back and breathe. Deeply breathe in and slowly let it out, allowing your exhale to be longer than your inhale. By taking deep, slow breaths, your body is forced to calm down. This is not a psychological trick but a physical reaction to your breathing.

3. Remember your why

Why are you doing this? What drives you to succeed? Why do you need this? What do you wish to gain from your business?

Whether you have your why written down, placed on a vision board, or hold it in your heart, keep your why at the forefront. I've heard many times, "does your why make you cry?" But I am going to ask you something different. Does your why make you smile? Does it drive you? Does it get you excited to jump out of bed?

A why that powerful will force you to push through your fears. I call this savage mode. I know this phrase sometimes has a negative connotation, but I refer to savage mode as a hyper-focused drive in which I take massive action with thick skin.

I think I gained this ability when I was a single mom living in low-income housing. As a single mom, you will do anything to feed your child and provide everything they need. You will put all of their needs before your own and are incredibly motivated to give them a better life than your own. You don't care what anyone thinks. You have thick skin and are a workhorse. This is the fight you need to drive you.

Embrace the Unknown

As George Addair said, "Everything you've ever wanted is sitting on the other side of fear." The most repeated command in the Bible is "Fear not!" It's been said that there are 365 "Fear nots"; one for every day of the year. But did you know fear is spoken over 500 times? God has methodically placed reminders repeatedly so we will lean on Him and not allow the fear to paralyze us.

Learn from your fear. Let it shape who you are. I know it is easier said than done, but try to welcome fear as an experience to learn and grow. The more you embrace the unknown, the more confidence you will gain. Besides, enthusiasm gives us the same physical reactions as fear, such as butterflies and feeling flush. Maybe you are just excited, and it's masquerading as fear. Either way, embrace it!

I am not asking you to be perfect, but I am asking you to take baby steps and do at least one thing that scares you. Living in your comfort zone is not living. By not facing your fears, you increase your fears, and eventually, they will take over your life. Instead, step out of your comfort zone and work on getting comfortable with being uncomfortable. Stop procrastinating and just do it scared. Commit to doing one thing every day that scares you and think of me asking you, "but did you die?"

Make the bold decision today not to let fear hold you back anymore. It won't happen overnight, but taking intentional action and running toward your fears daily will strengthen your courage muscles and shatter barriers. Remember, everything you want in life is just past your comfort zone.

3. THE CROWN FRUIT

The crown of a tree makes food to survive and bears beautiful fruit. However, the health of the tree, its environment, and its fruiting habits all influence its ability to produce fruit. Sound familiar?

Your physical, mental and spiritual health, the people you surround yourself with, and your daily habits influence your ability to produce fruit in your business. Learning and failing help in this production and are the most inspiring part of your success.

Fail Forward

When I was about to be a freshman in high school, I decided to try out for the dance team.

Many of my friends were trying out, and it seemed like a no-brainer with my dancing background. I started hearing how everyone on the team knew how to do the splits, and most could split left or right. I got nervous. I could split right but not left. I went to every practice leading up to the tryouts, often staying longer to perfect the dances and work on my flexibility. More buzz went around about what was expected as a dancer throughout the practices. I got scared. When it came to the day of tryouts, I showed up but left! I was too afraid to try out and fail, so I walked away.

My freshman year was filled with many FOMO (fear of missing out) and regrets. I felt like a failure for a long time. When tryouts came back around, I ignored the negative thoughts. I went to every practice, and this time, I didn`t just show up on tryout day. I TRIED OUT and, of course, made it. My high school years of dancing were some of my favorite memories. If I had let my fear determine my next steps, I wouldn`t have experienced that joy. I had to fail forward and learn to get there.

Failure is not the opposite of success; it`s a stepping stone on your path to your ultimate success. It is part of your growth. This is one of the hardest things to understand because the last thing we want to do is fail, especially in our business. The truth is, everyone fails. The biggest success stories include a lot of failures along the way.

Being a veteran in this industry for over 22 years, I can tell you I didn`t start successfully. In fact, I can confidently say I failed my way to the top. Each failure got me that much closer to the next step. Start looking at failure as a way to get to success faster.

Change is inevitable and is an opportunity, not an obstacle. If something is not working, pivot! Like the Ross 'pivot` moment in *Friends*, sometimes we need to adjust. Maybe what you are currently doing needs a bit of tweaking.

Be open to adapting to new things that come your way. It can be a powerful tool for your success. Even billion-dollar companies need to pivot sometimes. Adapting can save your struggling business, create new growth opportunities or be the breakthrough that allows for your ultimate success. Be open to change.

But Did You Die?

I hope each time you feel fear creep in or feel yourself being pulled away from the things that scare you, you think of me asking you, "but did you die?"

My greatest hope for you is that you send the message, ask the question, make the post, provide solutions, and/or share your opportunity. Be courageous! Fear may never go away, but it can change how you react to it. Face it, walk through it, learn from it and never let it stop you!

Coach's Notes: Jennifer started by talking about the phrase, "but did you die." She ended with the exact phrase. This phrase gives us so much perspective. Rich people think long term, whereas poor people think short term. This applies in all areas of your life. It applies spiritually, physically, mentally, and emotionally. Most of your so-called fears are just your brain protecting you from the worst-case scenario, which is so unlikely. When you understand this, you realize how it is worth going after those goals, dreams, and ambitions. My parting thought is this. Imagine you are really, really old. Let's say you are 100 years old, and you are on your deathbed. How laughable would it be to think you were once scared to make new invites because of fear????

"You can't have a testimony without a test or a message without a mess."

— Joyce Meyer

JUSTINE LAYSER

- Massive customer base personally selling over $300K annually.
- Has spoken and served on numerous panels at company conferences.
- Certified John Maxwell Speaker, Trainer & Coach.
- Certified DISC Facilitator & Enneagram Coach.

In the network marketing industry, reaching out for the first time to a prospective customer or business partner can be terrifying to many. The second most scary thing is following up and being seen as annoying or pushy.

Coach's Notes: Justine describes it perfectly. We are scared of being TOO pushy! I know I was. I was so scared of being perceived as pushy that I didn't follow up very well. Just remember the fortune is the follow upssssss. Yes, that's a typo, but on purpose, so

you don't miss the plural part. MULTIPLE FOLLOW UPS are KEY! Justine knows from experience that the fortune is in the follow-up process. This is one of the best follow-up systems I have ever seen.

When we keep in mind that only two percent of sales are made in the first contact, it becomes abundantly clear why following up is the way to become a successful closer. Failing to do so will result in missing out on ninety eight percent of your sales!!

This statistic shows us the importance of checking back in with each prospect. You can be a master at first reach outs, but you have wasted your time without a plan for following up!

Why should we want to become fanatical about follow-up?

1. People are BUSY! Often we assume that someone is being rude to us by not responding when what has actually happened is that the person just got distracted by something else that is more important or requires more immediate attention.

    Sometimes the prospect has the intention to purchase, join, or respond, and it just was not a convenient time, or the process was too involved, and it went to the bottom of their to-do list.

2. If we don't, someone else will! If you don't follow up with your prospect and someone else reaches out, and now this is the second, third or fourth touch, they are more likely to sign them up. The potential customer will not automatically return to you, the original point of contact! As a matter of fact, they rarely will!! This should make you put this book down and start following up immediately!!

3. Follow-up builds trust. People give business to people they know, like, and trust. By continuing to show up when you say you're going to and in a professional manner, you are showing them that you are a person of your word and that your products/business matter to you, and that you believe it should matter to them, too.

4. It's our job! It's a massive part of what we do. If you find yourself perpetually bothered because your prospects have entered the WPP (Witness Protection Program), understand that it is 100 percent normal. Still, it's also indicative that you aren't following up with enough people to have a whole funnel. You can't run a business like a hobby and expect to get million-dollar results. Your paycheck is a direct reflection of how many people you help. Since we already know people typically don't allow themselves to be helped until exposure #5, we have to learn the skills to do our job well.

We are so lucky to be in network marketing at a time when we can use social media. Social media gives us other ways to stay in front of our potential customers and not be forgotten. We can use our good, quality social media posts and story sequences. Tik Tok, Reels, and other short-form videos are "currently" a platform that is pushed in front of people. We can also interact with them on their social media posts just to stay front and center and "unforgettable," so when we do our follow-ups, they remember who we are and feel like they have a relationship with us!

Keep in mind that people are extremely busy and the world is SUPER NOISY! Follow-up is even more important now than ever, and it takes even more touches to stand out in a world filled with information and distractions.

Coach's Notes: We are indeed very lucky to have social media. It is a tool that can significantly enhance your business if you use it the right way and follow Justine's suggestions. Stay recallable. Social media is such an incredible way for people to remember you. It will bridge the gap between trust and credibility to help increase your results by inviting and following up.

Now that you know why it is essential to become fanatical at follow-up, it`s time to learn how! Here are the Six S`s of Fanatical Follow UP:

1. Set up the appointment

It`s so exciting! Either you have reached out to someone or vice versa, and you asked them if they are open to taking a look at your information, and they say YES! Often, we are so excited that we forget to set the appointment.

After you send a video or pdf and/or add them to a FB group and tag them in some information, it`s time to ensure that your prospect expects that you will be checking in with them.

Example: *"I will follow up with you to get all your questions asked. If I call/text/message/email you tomorrow at 8 pm, will you have had a chance to look at the info I sent to you?"*

If they ask for more time, honor that and come up with a mutually acceptable time. If they say 'yes,` a good response is: *"Great. I promise I will follow up at that time. I'll be setting a reminder. Maybe you will want to do the same. We will chat then!!"*

Setting up a time conveys respect and that you value your time and theirs. It shows professionalism and that you are serious about your business. The next step is to be sure that you follow up at exactly the time you agreed upon unless there is a major emergency in your life. If you have to cancel, give them plenty of notice and re-set the appointment. These actions show that you treat your business like a business and that you will do what you say!

2. Stop the verbal vomit

After you set the time, show up on time! Here is an example of how you can begin your first follow up conversation:

Hi (name)! I wanted to follow up with you just as I promised! Did you have a chance to watch the info/watch the video/ scroll through the group?

Answer: Yes, I did!

Fantastic! What did you like best about what you saw?

Or

Fantastic! How did the video/information make you feel?

Answer: No. I didn't have a chance.

When do you think you can commit to watching the video? It's only five minutes or option two Scroll through the group? It shouldn't take you more than ten minutes.

Set another appointment!! Same as before. Keep following this system until they look at the info.

When they tell you what they liked best or how they felt, find common ground with what they say. DO NOT REGURGITATE the info they have already looked at. Less is always more in this instance.

Examples:

I understand how you feel about being excited about what this can do for your life. I felt the same way when I first saw the info. What I found is that there is reason to be excited. This company is amazing! What questions do you have for me?

I understand how you feel about hesitancy with "miracle products." I felt the same way after trying so many that didn't work. I found that not only did I have fantastic results, but so are a lot of my friends and family. What other questions do you have?

When someone asks questions about products, answer the questions without giving more info than what they ask. Why? Because too many people talk themselves right out of a sale. They only need to know what THEY need to know. Verbal vomit is a killer. People are used to going to a store or virtual store and purchasing something without a long process of listening to someone's explanation. Keep it simple. Confused and overwhelmed people won't purchase.

Suppose a prospect has questions about the business, transition to a three-way chat as soon as possible. Third-party validation is always the most crucial step in growing a team. When we are excited about the possibility of a new teammate joining our team, many times, we just want to share all the info we know. But that can turn someone off. They don't want to learn all that info and believe that they will have to do whatever they see you do. If it seems complicated or overwhelming, they will have no interest in adding that to their lives. By piquing a prospect's interest and then introducing them to a teammate, you're able to avoid the issue of verbal vomit. With this process they will learn that they don't need to know everything about the products & company to run their business.

Suppose you do not receive a response when you follow up. Don't be surprised. Don't get upset. Don't be angry. It often happens, so just expect it. Life happens. Usually, it is not personal or deliberate. Stay in control of your emotions and the process, and continue to act as a professional.

Example (about 3-4 days after the scheduled follow up):

I'm sorry it has taken me so long to hop back in here with you. Business has been crazy busy. How's everything going with you?

If they respond...set up the appointment again.

If there is still no response, after about two to three more days:

I know you're super busy, and I don't want to keep bothering you. I just want to make sure that I answer all your questions before you decide to move forward or move on.

In the meantime, be sure to interact with their social media. Comment on posts, stories, reels, tik toks. You want your name to pop up and remain in their mind.

If after six or seven more days you still haven't heard from them, the following message almost always prompts a response:

I hope you're OK. I'm starting to get worried about you.

No one wants you to worry. This is a fantastic way to get back into the conversation. Many times you will learn that the prospect had an emergency situation. Sometimes they were just overwhelmed with life and busy. Again, it is very rarely personal.

It's time to determine if they are still interested. If so, re-set the appointment and continue with the process.

If they have changed their mind, simply ask if you can follow up again in six months to see if their circumstances have changed. If the answer is yes, be sure to get their name in whatever planning system you use.

3. Solve their problem

Some will say yes. Some will be on the fence. Give them an answer to their problem. As the follow-up process goes from one appointment to the next, prospects often mention hesitations and ask more questions.

Examples:

I'm not sure that it will work. I've tried so many different products.

—I'll tag you in another testimony in the FB group I added you to.

I don't have very many friends/I don't know many people.

*Facts tell. Stories sell. – **I have heard other people say the same thing. I've got to tell you about my friend, ___. She told me a similar thing a few years ago.*** *(tell ___ story)*

I don't have enough time.

*—**Oh my word! I have to introduce you to my friend, ___. She is the busiest person I know. She started with us __ years/ months ago and she has already _____.***

When people don't see a way for something to work, validating their feelings is a way to make a connection. After sharing a story, tagging them in a testimony, or finding common ground, if there are still hesitations, the next step is to set up the next appointment: ***It seems like you may need more information. I'd like to_____.***

—share a pdf about our compensation plan.

—have you check out our opportunity webinar tomorrow night.

—hop on the phone with you at a time that works for both of us.

—send you information about our ingredients.

—invite you to our special FB group.

—introduce yourself to someone I think will resonate with what you're going through.

Keep setting appointments until you get a solid 'yes' or 'no.' Too often we think the process should be fast. Remember, sixty percent of customers reject our offers the first four times. We are simply taking our prospects from exposure to exposure until we get an answer. Make every effort to get them enough info and the type of info they need to help them decide one way or another.

This is a business. So be sure to stay in control and keep in mind that we are offering them a product or business to help them. We are attempting to help them solve a problem in their life.

If the process seems too drawn out, either you or the 'expert' in your three-way chat can ask a simple question to find out where the potential stands.

On a scale of 1-10, with one being not at all and ten being... I'm all in; where would you say you are with your decision.

If the answer is four or below: *I understand. What is holding you back?*

If the answer is 5 or 6, they need validation.

Suppose the answer is seven or above: *Fantastic! It sounds like you're ready to get started.*

If, at any time in the process of solving their problem, the prospect says 'no.' We always ask if we can follow up at a later date. *Would you mind if I check back with you in X months to see if your circumstances have changed?*

4. Seek a response

Asking for a decision is all about posture. Many prospects will simply not tell you they are ready if you do not very directly ask them for the sale or to join. This is highly uncomfortable for many reps in MLM. But it is part of our 'job.'

—From what you're telling me, it seems like you're ready to get started? Would you like to know what info I need to set you up?

Or

So do you see an opportunity for you and your family?

Or

Do you see this system as a way to reach your goals?

Or

It sounds like this is a good fit for your financial problems.

Make this all about them. Focus on solving the problems of your prospect. Success in the follow-up is not about always making a sale. It is always about the prospect and how you can help them and create a relationship with them. Whenever you can provide value to another person and become a person who is seen as able to solve problems, you set yourself up for future success.

5. Shift the conversation

Whether someone ignores your messages or says they are not interested, it gives you the perfect opportunity to shift the conversation to ask for a referral. But instead of simply asking for the referral, we are using the takeaway and the referral.

You will agree with them that 'this is not a good fit' (or a good time) for him/her, then share a win that you recently had in your business or with your products and ask if they know someone who would love to win just like you did!!

The takeaway is effective because no one wants to be literally or figuratively crossed off a list. People hate not to be considered for something that they know is beneficial to them or that they can imagine themselves doing and believe in the potential for their success.

Another approach is if you have a new teammate or customer experience something positive, ask your prospect if they know someone with a similar background.

Example:

I just brought on a new rockstar teammate who is a stay-at-home parent/personal trainer/teacher who achieved XYZ. Do you know any SAHMs who may be interested in doing the same?

Don't verbal vomit!! Don`t try to re-recruit. Simply state what you`re looking for and leave it at that. FOMO (fear of missing out) may make them curious enough to ask questions.

A more generic way to shift the conversation and swing back around is to say something like this:

I wanted to pop in and say hello. I have a quick question for you, but first, how are things with you? (or a more personal question)

Then

I know people's circumstances change in life, and I don't know if that holds true for you or not, but I wanted to see if maybe this is a better time for you to look at or consider what it is I've been doing (or XYZ product).

6. Strengthen your posture

Know that you have a phenomenal opportunity and products. Be confident in your offer and how you present it. One teammate or customer will not make or break your future. Your job is not to convince. It is to share information and guide them through the process as they determine the best path for them.

Never leave the next reach out in the hands of your prospect. ninety nine percent of the time, they will not initiate the follow-up conversation. It`s 100 percent your responsibility, and the way you show up to the next follow-up with them will have a lot to do with the outcome. Your posture, confidence, and ability to remove yourself from the outcome and focus solely on what your prospect needs will serve you well.

Follow-up is the number one most important skill you need to learn in network marketing. Without the learned skills of follow-up, you will find closing almost non-existent. Get in the habit of following up with a set number of people each day or intensely on a specific day(s) of the week. For example; some people find it easiest to remember to do the activity on Friday because it is Follow Up Friday. Many people find that prospects are in a better and more hopeful mood on Friday because, for many, it is payday, and they tend to purchase and join businesses at a higher rate on that day.

As far as the organization of prospects, there are many different ways to organize your follow-up. Some examples are the more traditional 3x5 card and notebook systems with color-coded highlighters and more techy options like apps that can aid you in prioritizing who needs to be messaged. Some popular apps are to-do-list, TickTick, Any.do or google tasks/calendar.

Follow-up simply has to happen. It`s a non-negotiable in our businesses.

Becoming fanatical about follow-up will pay you dividends in your business!! Follow-up is simply maintaining contact with a prospect to determine if your business opportunity or products are able to solve their problem. These tips will become more natural and easy to navigate with time and practice.

Coach's Notes: All success is a process. All success will take time. Don't be discouraged when you struggle with the follow-up. As you consistently practice Justine's follow-up system, you will notice subtle improvements which will eventually lead to massive changes. She has taken years of failures and successes to create a system you can follow. The most challenging parts of success are, first, knowing what to do. And second, actually implementing what you know you should be. Let's implement the follow-up system!

"First we make our habits, and then our habits make us."

— John Dryden

LESLEY WEISS ZWICK

- Top .01% of my network marketing company.

- 6 figure earner within 1 year.

- Went from extreme debt to the ability to move our family to our dream destination.

- Now building a mindset coaching business in addition to my network marketing business.

The 3 Super Powers of Building your Business: Willpower, Thrill-Power, and Skill-Power

Superheros. In my house, they are all the rage. My kids are OBSESSED. But what really makes someone a superhero? What gives someone superpowers? So many of the superheroes we hear about have crazy powers. They can fly, have super strength, can freeze things, and read minds...but what if I were to tell you WE ALL have superpowers?!?! What if I were to tell you that learning how to tap into them can completely transform your life AND your network marketing business? That time is NOW, and ANYONE can become super in their own lives and in their own business! So, what's the secret?

First off, I want to start by getting rid of the idea of needing to be a "HERO" to be SUPER. Having a superpower does not mean you have to be a superhero. In all honesty, a HERO is the last thing we want to be! If you need a hero, that means there are always the opposite points on the triangle (the drama triangle), the VICTIM and the VILLAIN, and when we are building a business or anything in our lives for that matter, we don't want the victim or villain options to even be in our realm of possibilities. Instead, I want to change your method of thinking to a much more powerful triangle; one that has three points that help us BUILD and use our superpowers. These three points are made up of THE CREATOR, THE CHALLENGER, and THE COACH! So, from now on, we will be SUPER-CREATORS!

So what are these 3 SUPERPOWERS that help us build our businesses and our lives, and how do we get them?? The great thing is EVERYONE who wants them has them! These powers are WILLPOWER, SKILL-POWER, and THRILL-POWER!

These three powers together are the secret sauce behind all success. The truth is, we all already use them, but are you using them INTENTIONALLY?

Coach's Notes: I love how Lesley is talking about superheroes. I believe that we are all born with some of our superpowers and some of our superpowers are skills that we work on mastering. We can all be SUPER like Lesley mentioned by working on personally developing skill sets that will make a

difference in our lives, and the lives of people around us. As you continue to read this chapter, read the three superpowers that Lesley is talking about and ask yourself, "Is this something I already have, or is this something that I need to acquire?"

Let's start with **WILLPOWER**.

Willpower. EVERYTHING starts with willpower. We have a WANT, and we put our nose to the grindstone to get it.

Want to lose weight? You need the WILLPOWER to stick to your food plan. Want to clean up your finances? You need WILLPOWER to refrain from making impulse purchases. Want to do well in school? You need the WILLPOWER to get your work done even when there are other fun things tempting you. Want to build your network marketing business? You need the WILLPOWER to do the work it requires. There is no way around it…WILLPOWER to start is important, otherwise all of the other temptations will win EVERY. SINGLE. TIME.

Six years ago I was physically, emotionally, and financially a mess. I was seventy five pounds overweight, depression and anxiety controlled my decisions. We were deep in debt, barely able to keep food on the table and a roof over our heads. I needed a change. I had to decide WHAT to change first. I chose my physical health since that was how I could see a path to health in other areas of my life. Starting took WILLPOWER. Those first few days were tough; breaking the sugar addiction and not having my regular ways to cope with anxiety (food was my drug of choice). I will tell you, I have VERY, VERY little WILLPOWER. Had that been my only superpower, I would have quit on myself quickly.

The same came about when I started my business. Drowning in debt, my need for an income was strong. So my willpower to follow the structure laid out in front of me was in full force. The temptation of making my own hours and working when I wanted was VERY enticing. But, the financial needs and wants of my family ignited my willpower.

Coach's Notes: Every single truly successful individual has found a way to muster that willpower. For the unsuccessful I get that it can be daunting at first. This is why Lesley teaches you to start SMALL. Small little wins of willpower help you exercise the WILLPOWER muscle. It will give you confidence you can do more and you will eventually build up to doing much harder things. If you aren't a runner no one would tell you to go start by running a marathon. You would start small. You may even start with running less than a mile on day one and even some walking during that time. The main point is that willpower is a MUST for you to have success so start small and build up.

Once WILLPOWER is in full swing, super power number two comes into play. THRILL-POWER is often a positive side effect of WILLPOWER. THRILL-POWER is the feeling of getting quick results. For example, when it comes to weight loss it's when those first few pounds fall off, your energy begins to soar, clothing starts to get loose, etc. In business, it's the thrill of your first client or customer, the thrill of your first paycheck, the thrill of being recognized by your team or your upline.

THRILL-POWER is what keeps us going when our starting willpower is dying. THRILL-POWER is the incentive to keep moving forward and is what helps us create habit loops. We want more of the THRILL, so we keep doing the actions that provide it.

But, let`s be real here....THRILL-POWER dies as well. We get comfortable when we fall into the "fine" zone. Slowly things creep back in such as old habits, and/or old routines come back. We often don`t notice them until we`ve gone way too far, and then it feels almost impossible to come back. Have you ever felt that way? If you have, then you know what comes next....we often go on to the "next best thing,"...and we quit on ourselves. But honestly, quitting is not the answer, it`s the drama cycle that we all desperately want to break out of but aren`t sure how.

So how do we prevent this?? THAT is the MILLION DOLLAR QUESTION, and it`s answered by building POWER number three, SKILL-POWER!

WILLPOWER comes from a decision. THRILL-POWER comes as the response to that decision. SKILL-POWER is a combination of both, and it`s truly the glue that holds the entire package together. SKILL-POWER is the secret sauce that separates those who are successful and those who are not.

SKILL-POWER takes intention, practice and messing up so you can grow. It takes being honest with yourself, consistency and work. When you are ready for it, it`s magical!

So, how do we build SKILL-POWER? **One.Day.At.A.Time**. We start with simple things. We start by looking at the actions we are taking to get the THRILL and examining how we can do them with consistency, one small action at a time.

Let's take the SKILL-POWER of starting good conversations on Social Media for business building. That skill first starts by doing it (WILLPOWER). When people respond to your message, you get the THRILL of building the relationship. The SKILL comes in when you sit down and ask yourself questions about these conversations. Are you asking good questions to get to know the person you are talking to, or are you simply engaging so you can check the task off on a list your upline gave you? If it's the latter you won't get very far, and the THRILL will disappear quickly.

SKILL building is slow. But when you do it and look back six weeks, six months, or even six years later, you will see how far all of those tiny baby steps have taken you.

So how do we put this all into action?? How do we start?

Newton's Law of Physics states an object in motion STAYS in motion, an object at rest stays at rest! The same is true for your business. The great thing is, no matter how long you've been in business, it's never too early or too late to start!

Top 5 ACTION STEPS to start TODAY

1. GET IN ACTION! Fire up your willpower. If you aren't in steady motion, go back to WHY you got into your business. Make a list of all the things you love about it, what you want to accomplish, and take action.

Those steps are as simple as starting a new conversation on FB, putting up a post on social media, or calling a past client/customer. This first step can be tiny; it's simply a step. Taking this step ignites a power in our brain that gets us moving!

2. Know your company's trends. Is this a good time of year or a tough time of year for your company? IF it's a tough time, DO NOT use that as an excuse...use it as momentum towards your action plan. If you're not working through the tough times, you won't be ready for the BOOM that happens later. Your daily business growth IS NOT a reflection on what you did that day, but instead on what you've been doing in the past. Tough times in our business are the best time to build relationships and practice our SKILLS!

3. SEEK the THRILL! Every day document the WINS in your life. Both big things and small things. What we focus on is what grows. WINS do not and should not be just about business and instead include all areas of your life.

4. Evaluate your skills. What are you really good at? What skills in your business do you need help with? Once you identify these, you can then set a plan of action to improve. Stink at putting up good engaging stories panels? Make a daily action plan to do a few days and ask for feedback. Are you AMAZING at creating power posts on Facebook? Teach someone else how to do it to hone your skills! We improve our skills when we teach them to others. Who can you mentor, and who can mentor you?

5. Create your plan for when life happens. Create your list of ACTIONS that you can do every day, even on your worst day! USE YOUR SKILLS. The more you use them, the more you will fire up your willpower and skill-power.

NOW...Go out there and HAVE FUN! If you aren't having fun in this business, you're doing it all wrong!

Coach's Notes: I love the five actions step because it gives you a set plan. Number one is the most important because it is where most network marketers fail. As Lesley goes through steps two, five notice how she is now teaching the value of being deliberate with your time. She is teaching how to take action. She is teaching you to maximize your time. Time is the most valuable thing we have on this earth. Use it wisely.

LESLEY WEISS ZWICK

"Be thankful for what you have; you'll end up having more. If you concentrate on what you don't have, you will never, ever have enough."

– Oprah Winfrey

LISA S. HILL

- First-time network marketer from Savannah, GA, currently resides in Metro Atlanta, GA, with her husband.

- Joined her company in 2013. She encourages her team, The Heavy Hitters, to #DreamBig #DreamBoldly #DreamInColor, and #DreamWithoutLimits Her goal is to continue showing her team the limits we have are the ones we place on ourselves.

- Computer Technology Specialist of 13 years.

- Leads a team of over 127,000 consultants.

- Six-Figure Earner Award four consecutive years in a row.

Coach's Notes: It is estimated that there are more introverts than extroverts in network marketing. I have a friend who did 70,000 surveys and gave me this insight. That's absolutely crazy! Both Lisa and I are examples of introverts who made it in this business. If

you aren't an introvert, please pay attention because you will want to learn this content to share with the introverts that join your team.

Four Tips On How To Overcome Being An Introvert

One of the biggest misconceptions I see in network marketing is that people believe that only extroverts who love being in big crowds and love talking to people can build a successful business.

Believe it or not, I am an introvert. I don't mind attending social gatherings, but if there are too many people attending...I will be ready to go! I call this being a social introvert. I'm comfortable with being invited out and attending social events, but there are those moments when I want to run back to my safe place and get in my comfy clothes and chill. While many of us introverts don't mind socializing, we just prefer small groups as too many people are overwhelming for us. I will share with you the top ten tips about how introverts can be successful in network marketing.

1. Step Out Of Your Comfort Zone and enter your Growth Zone

Everything we want is outside of our comfort zone. It is in our comfort zone where we become stagnant. We have to be willing to step outside of our comfort so that we are open to meeting new people. This doesn't haven't to be extravagant, and it doesn't have to be hard. We can step outside of our comfort zone by joining groups on social media that include our hobbies. We can start by making one or two comments on new people's posts. Stepping out of your comfort zone may be getting in front of a room to share your story or being more transparent in your posts. You may want to speak up on your team page or even offer to lead a team meeting. These are easy ways to get outside the comfort zone and start to see that making connections doesn't have to be hard. To step outside your comfort zone, you will have to remember WHY you want to do this. When you start network marketing, you will have many examples of successful people. You will see what they have and maybe want that too. Remember, every person you see who is successful is consistently stepping outside of their comfort zone.

As an introvert myself, I found the hardest part of this business was becoming more transparent and moving from being a social media scroller to a social media author. It felt like I was being too exposed to share personal things on social media. BUT, I also knew that the posts that I loved the most were the authentic people. I couldn't stay stuck playing small any longer. If you want to do things in a new way, you will want to step outside your self-imposed box. In my business, we like to say, Show it, Wear it and Join us! Show the product, show you using your product. Show the success that your product can bring to those who follow the blueprint.

Coach's Notes: Stepping out of your comfort zone is soooo hard for most introverts! Most believe they need to become extroverts to succeed, which isn't true. Your goal is to become the boldest version of you, which will look completely different from anyone else. Once you realize this and focus on it, getting out of your comfort zone is much easier.

2. Silence Your Inner Critics

We often kill our dreams and drive when we underestimate our power. We kill any of our success just by thinking and getting in our way. As introverts, sometimes we feel that we can't be successful because we think it has to look a certain way and know that's not us. We get in our heads and our own ways. Did you know that each and every one of us has two voices inside our heads? One of the voices is confidence, and one of the voices is self-doubt. Our voice of confidence is the one that motivates us. The one of self-doubt is the one that discourages us. It's no surprise that none of us make any money when we are listening to the voice of self-doubt.

Stop comparing yourself to others. Remove the negative thoughts that we can't be successful because we don't have a network, or because we are afraid to share the opportunity. There is someone who needs this opportunity just like us. We can't be afraid to share about it, or they may never get their own chance. We need to stop listening to the self-doubt and stop being afraid to speak with them. There is a whole community out there just like us needs this opportunity. Some people want extra money, and maybe that extra money could make all of the difference to them. How are you allowing the fear of meeting new people hold you back?

We have to place ourselves in the spotlight and show them that we are strong and courageous to speak with a stranger. We have to find those people and share our stories of how to overcome and let them know they can too. We have to be the positive person in the room who shines light and lets people know that they can also have this. There is a saying, "birds of a feather flock together." I know that's true. If you want success, you have to start hanging around successful people. You want to be seeing what they do, hearing how they talk, and even implementing what they are doing. When you silence the inner critic, you will watch your circle of influence grows.

3. Set small goals to build your confidence while interacting in social settings

As I mentioned before, you don't have to change everything today. Start small. I often see people get frozen in overwhelm when they see successful people and then judge themselves against them. They say things like, "I could never get on stage like that." Or, "I would never be able to talk to that many people." Good news! I don't expect you to. At least not today! Learning to talk with people and interact more with others is a skill set that can be worked on bit by bit. It doesn't take talking to one hundred people every day to build this business. It takes small actionable steps every single day consistently. I want you to write down where you think you are right now. If we go back to my example of me on social media, I first needed to know how I interacted on social media. So I might write down something like, "on social media scrolling every day. Post on major holidays, and never my face." That is a good start! I have to know where I am before knowing how to go where I want to. The next step would be to set a small goal. In this example, a small goal might be, "Post every two weeks, and once a month, post a picture of myself." Set small goals, and track them.

4. Face your FEAR

Writing this chapter wasn't easy for me. Even knowing that I wouldn't have to see anyone didn't make it any easier. It is hard to put myself out there and share with millions of people that I don't know. It doesn't matter if I am becoming an author and writing for the first time, or turning on the camera for a Facebook live in front of a small group of strangers and friends; I have learned a trick that has helped me face my fears. A business partner taught me this several years ago, which has helped me ever since. Take a moment before you do anything that makes you afraid, and have fun! Make silly faces at the camera, laugh aloud before you sit to write the first sentence in the chapter, or even dance for a whole song while singing at the top of your lungs. Fears are scary because we take them so seriously. Quit saying you are trying to overcome your fears and loosen it up a bit. Quit judging yourself and your audience, thinking that everyone is thinking badly about you. Not everyone is, and not everything is serious all of the time.

Another thing I like to do that helps me face my fears is to find affirmations that help center and ground me into remembering who I am. I speak those affirmations repeatedly to help me remind myself that I am loved, I am awesome, and I have something to contribute. As I write those affirmations, they help me feel grounded and peaceful.

Not everyone in network marketing is an extrovert. You can have huge success in this business and in life while being an introvert. When I was learning how to push past the scary things and talk to new people, I made a list of people that are famous introverts. Anytime I doubted myself or thought that success just wasn't for us introverts, I would pull out my list and remind myself that some of the most successful people are introverts. Here is the list; you can read this repeatedly if you need some inspiration....our very own Rob Sperry, along with Michael Jordan, Michael Jackson, J.K. Rowling, Christina Aguilera, Bill Gates, and President Barack Obama to name a few. All of these people are successful introverts. They worked on their confidence, built deep relationships with others, and continued to be persistent in believing that anything was possible for them. Just think, there is another introvert watching you and waiting for you to show them that they can do this too.

As you finish this chapter, I want to share this poem with you:

The World of Introverts

Yes, I`m an introver.t

No, I`m not stuck up.

No I`m not antisocial.

I`m just listening. I`m just observing.

I can`t stand small talk... but I`ll talk about life for hours.

I`d rather be home with a close friend or two than among a big crowd of acquatninences.

Don`t scold me in public.

Don`t embarrass me in public.

Respect that I`m reserved.

And if I open myself up to you,

Know that means you`re very special to me.

~Author Unknown

Coach's Notes: As Lisa said, "'face your fear." She has a poem to help her. I had a power statement that I secretly created that I had to read fifteen times a day to empower me to overcome my fears. I had a dream board, and I listened to books every day to help me become stronger mentally and overcome my massive fears. Surround yourself with whatever you need to help you overcome your fears.

LISA S. HILL

"Our greatest glory is not in never falling, but in rising every time we fall"

— Confucius

LAURA CAROFFINO

- Over $600 Million in lifetime group volume sales within five years.
- Top .001% income earner.
- Multiple seven-figure earner.
- Multiple trip earner.
- Public speaker and trainer.

PURPOSE AND PASSION

Throughout the different phases of my life, I have always been driven in my life by purpose and passion. As an intel analyst working for the Pentagon, I was passionate about my career and felt completely purpose-driven in the work I was doing. I loved working for the Department of Defense and was engaged in the relevant work of field research. I stayed committed to my career even after I met and married my husband, who was in the Marine Corps and was stationed worldwide. But then, something happened. I started to question my purpose. My passion started to fade. With me in D.C. at the Pentagon, and my new husband stationed in California, something felt off. We became tired of living apart.

This is important for all of us to understand. Passion and purpose change throughout the years. We may have something that lights us up and has us jumping out of bed in the morning. But as time goes on and our circumstances change, that passion and purpose will ebb and flow. I knew that as much as I loved my career, my relationship and my husband meant more to me than all of the work I was doing for the Intelligence Community.

As I left the industry, I wondered if I would ever find something as fulfilling or something that could replace the income I was making. For the time being, I decided I would focus on being a stay-at-home mom with our then three small children at the time. I went from career woman to full-time mom, and it was one of the most difficult transitions I have ever been through.

Have you ever had a transition like that? One that you knew in your heart was the right decision because it aligns with your passion and purpose, but is hard to make because of the sacrifices you will be making? We all face tough choices. This is one reason that knowing your passion and purpose is important. This will help guide you through decisions and help you to make sacrifices, even when it feels hard.

So after quitting my career and staying home with the kids, I realized that I also needed something for me to feel like me again. It felt like the passion and purpose were gone. I know some of your parents, especially moms, can relate. I felt like my identity was lost with just being a stay-at-home mom. Don`t get me wrong, stay-at-home moms are amazing. They are. I felt blessed to be able to have that fantastic opportunity, but sometimes we as moms need a little bit more to feel like we need a little something outside of taking care of our kids.

Coach's Notes: Laura is a powerful story of an extremely busy Mom. She has five kids under the age of eighteen and a young baby. Think about it. So many of our brains create excuses on why we will never have success. We justify others have better personalities or more time. We justify others have better timing. Always look for ways to win rather than reasons to justify your future losses. Get your hopes up! This world loves to say don't get your hopes. I say the complete opposite. Your odds of success are always higher when you focus on your goals with an I CAN attitude.

I stumbled upon network marketing. I had taken my kids to get their hair cut at a salon and found a catalog I could look at while I waited. Everything in that catalog got my attention, and I called the person's number on the back. I think the woman I called was shocked that placing a catalog in a hair salon had gotten someone interested! I decided I would start looking for something that I could do from home because paying for a sitter or anything of that nature was just out of the question for our family.

I realized that her business was a "work from home" business, and I was intrigued. I thought that was the neatest concept ever. I had never heard of it or anything of that nature. I joined, and I did parties all the time through that concept. I earned enough to pay our car payments, which got me so excited that I started to think about how this business could be the new passion and purpose in my life. I was also desperate for some camaraderie with other adults and having something to talk about besides our kids. I wanted to feel that purpose and passion outside of my identity as a parent. Network marketing gave me all of that! This is the industry where I became a stay-at-home mom AND a working businesswoman. It finally felt like the best of both worlds for me.

It's EASIER than you think

As I started to make money in my business, I noticed something in the company I was working for. Several people were making six figures a year! This was huge for me. When I heard more and more that people were making great money, I thought, "If they can do this, I can too." That one thought led me to do the next step in my business. I started utilizing the best tool out there, a search engine.

At the time, Google was just starting to become popular. Now obviously, Google`s the biggest search engine out there, but there are so many different avenues you can use. You can start your business with less than you think you need. You can start by picking a search engine and creating content there. Think about YouTube. All you need is a camera that you can record and a computer to upload your video. That`s it!

You can also utilize those search engines to research everything about network marketing and direct sales to learn all the things. There`s a lot of free information out there. And that`s what I did to get where I am. I now run a nine-figure organization. This didn`t happen overnight. This was years of work and networking. But it started with a thought, "If they can do this, I can too." Start before you are ready, and don`t spend all of your time preparing to prepare for the day you feel ready. Jump in and start sharing.

Use what you got!

The other tool that I have found that really helped me was the free training that my company offered. You want to work smarter, not harder, so set time for pieces of training that you can do for ten minutes a day. You may want to stick with your company training initially because it gives you something to focus on directly. The company has done the research, and they are invested in your success. Take advantage of that and use what you got! So often, people think they have to reinvent the wheel. You don`t. Especially when it comes to training, you need to be focusing on consistency. Stay consistent in using what you got.

Doing the company training that was offered helped me not only learn more about the product, but it helped learn how to build a business, work on my personal development, build a team, and other leadership skills. Don`t underestimate what you can get done in ten minutes a day of training. I look back on what I have accomplished as I went all-in on myself and dedicated time to training. I can see that all areas of my life have improved because of my commitment to myself. I have been able to build friendships, learned how to build a legacy, no longer trade time for money, and how to work my work schedule around my family life. I have also learned how to fail forward and learn from my mistakes. All of this is because I have been willing to invest in training and then take the time to apply what I have learned.

Coach's Notes: As Laura said, consistency is the key. Yes, it can be boring, but it is so worth it. To have success, you must master consistency. No, that doesn't mean you need to be perfect. Of course, you will have setbacks. As you learn to create a reassociation to know that consistency is only helping you get closer to your goals, it will become more exciting. Learn to make the boring exciting, and your business will change dramatically.

Ask the right questions

I remember at the beginning of my business; I was so excited to get started that I spammed many people. I lost friends because of spamming, which was a hard lesson to learn. But I remember being so excited and thinking that everyone needed this right now that I didn't stop to think about how to introduce this to people and how what I was offering would help them. I had friends unsubscribe from my newsletter and stop following me on social platforms. It was hard, and my feelings were hurt. But I realized something through that experience. I had never once stopped to ask the right questions to myself or others.

So what are the right questions? First, you want to ask yourself some questions to see where you are and why you are doing what you are doing. Some of the questions could be:

- "What do I want to share? The product or opportunity?"
- "Why do I want to share it with this person?"
- "What am I doing wrong? What am I doing right?"
- "What is keeping people from saying yes?"
- "How am I showing up that keeps people from saying yes?"

When you can start to ask the right questions, you will start to find that you get out of fear of rejection or being upset that people aren't saying yes, and you start to see it as something to improve and get better at. When I started asking myself the right questions, I started diving into where I could improve and focus on that instead of getting down on myself.

Next, you can start asking other people the right questions. Instead of focusing on the sale, you can focus on where they are at and how you can best support or help them right now. Here are a couple of questions to consider.

- "What is tough in your life right now?"
- "Where are you interested in improvement in your life?"

- "Where would extra income make a difference in your life?"

- If you could achieve an extra $1,400 a month, what would change for you and your family?"

- "Would you be interested in learning how to make money or use a product that could improve your life?"

- "What would you need to achieve to create the desired lifestyle you and your family want?"

When I joined my current company five years ago, I knew that it would be a short-term adjustment for me and what I was bringing in. I looked back at the right questions to ask and answered them for myself. I realized that I would need to come up with $1,400 extra a month to pay for my children's private school education. This felt a bit daunting at the time because I was with a new company. I put it into my mind that I would need to figure this out, and I got to work. I kept believing that the $1,400/month was doable the first month and that belief and asking the right questions helped catapult my business forward. I was able to do that, plus some. So keep asking the right questions. Keep answering the questions and using those answers to take action in your business.

Building through adversity

As much as I would love to tell you that this fairy tale adventure has been all rainbows and unicorns, it hasn't. But that doesn't mean that I haven't been able to be successful. Do not let your limitations and set backs hold you back.

In 2018 I was hospitalized for six months. The doctor told me I had advanced stages of mixed connective tissue disease, which basically means the connective tissue around my heart and other organs was failing, and that my life expectancy would be anywhere from six months to six years. I was devastated, and I couldn't stop thinking about what that meant for myself and my family. I remember sitting there for three days and processing the news. I felt this great mourning for myself and what I wouldn't be able to do. But then, because of all of my work on myself, a thought came to my mind that changed everything. I thought, "I can do all things." That included facing this disease and whatever it brought with it.

Never allow your mind to stay stuck in fear. Yes, you will face fear and disappointment. We all do. But remember that you can rise above. As I rose out of this challenging period of time, it felt like I got knocked down again when I contracted a chronic bacterial infection. I had to pause once again and think about how I wanted to approach this. Surely anyone would understand if I decided to feel sorry for myself and tap out. But I decided that wasn't me, and that isn't how I wanted to face my life and the adversities I was facing. I took control of my situation and chose to face my condition my way with positive affirmations, lots of research, and doing things that made sense for me, even if it went against my doctor's opinions.

I share all of this with you because I saw so many connections between this time of my life and building a business. You will have things come at you that you weren't expecting. Some of them feel devastating. Not getting enough sales, having your company go under, switching companies, having your team quit! All of these feel hard, and no one wants to face them. But how you decide to approach them matters. It is absolutely a choice that you get to make. Through this period in my life, I decided to tell myself daily, "I will recover. I will overcome this." This helped me focus on what I could and take my healing very seriously.

I will recover. I will overcome this. Those are my daily affirmations that I tell myself to help me persevere. Even when I ended up being hospitalized for months, I maintained a high rank in my company. I asked people for help, and I was able to continue to work on my business and help other people as well. This was a choice! You get to choose how you show up for your own hard. As I mentioned before, I wish it was easy for all of us, but it isn`t. I still struggle with my health every single day. But I choose every single day how I will face it.

Conclusion

This business has been a game-changer for my family. I look back on what I thought my life would look like, and I could never have imagined where we are today. We have truly created a lifestyle and experiences that I had never thought were possible for us. It all was created because I decided to go all-in on myself. I decided to believe that I could be the person on stage. I believed that I could be the person to help others. No one can go after your dreams for you. It will have to be you. So go out, and make it happen regardless of what you face. Your dreams are waiting.

Coach's Notes: So many people misinterpret attraction marketing. Laura just taught you how to do it authentically. She taught you how to create your brand in a simple way. By focusing on social media the right way, you will see a noticeable difference with your audience. Let me give you an example. If you follow Laura's strategy and create some attraction marketing but don't have many people reaching out to you, here is what will happen that most don't think about. Let's say prior to attraction marketing, you were inviting twenty people to look at your business or products, and only about four would look. If you master attraction marketing, you will start to build trust with your audience, and that ratio can quickly go from four out of twenty taking a look to ten out of ten taking a look at your business or products. If you compound those numbers, it will make a MASSIVE impact on your business. Attraction marketing works if you work.

For I know the plans I have for you, *"declares the LORD," plans to prosper you and not to harm you, plans to give you hope and a future.*

— Jeremiah 29:11

LORI BENSON

- Been in the network marketing industry for eight years and had tremendous success in the first year. That success continues into the present.

- Has generated a seven-figure income for the last few years and has been able to obtain a six-figure income since the first year.

- Along with her team, she consistently generates approximately 24,000,000 in sales annually.

- Has had over one hundred team members enroll with her and two other team members in one single weekend by using the systems she designed for network marketing.

- Attributes her success to being consistent and following through with her own goals and helping others with a plan to launch their business.

Coach's Notes: Sponsoring is great, but you will eventually burn out if you don't have any duplication. The first step is to sponsor which is a great start but to hit the next ranks in your company you will need to learn how to launch a team member. In the beginning, it can be overwhelming but don't stress it. We all start as amateurs. Lori will lay out the strategies for becoming better at launching new team members.

Launching a new team member

We all start in this business with different experiences of "launching" into this business. When launching a team member, you want to know their level of interest and desire. We tend to think everyone operates on our level, which is simply not the case. Most team members join to be very part-time, and you want to create systems they can do in thirty minutes to one hour daily to see some results. It's important to know where people are at when they start this business because we all have different commitment levels and hours that we are willing to invest. Of course, to see more income requires more work.

The first step in launching a new team member is to talk to the new team member and listen to their goals and desires. Your job is to figure out and ask questions to know why they started this business so that you can help them along the way with their goals. My goal was to make six figures in one year, but that isn't most people's goal. When they begin, they just want to pay for their product or make $500, so everything needs to be geared towards that level, and you can expand from there.

Next, you want to design a game plan that fits your company's goals. The outcome that you are trying to achieve is to help the newest person obtain a few customers. It can be challenging for someone who has never done this to speak the language to enroll reps, so help them with a belief by enrolling a few customers. The faster you can get at helping people have success, the more willing they will be to stick to it, and start to see the potential in this business. Social media platforms are a great way to help people reach out and find people to make offers to, but remember, platforms often change, so be flexible in your marketing plans as it evolves.

This is a step that most people don't think about, but it is one of the most crucial steps! You must create a support chat with your new team member. This support chat will involve you, and one or two others in your team to help support the new team member. They will use this chat as an ongoing chat moving forward in the business. Group chats are for announcements, tips, sharing success, and positivity. Don't allow team members to use the group chat for complaints and negativity. The group chat gives people a dedicated spot to ask questions and get support. It also helps them feel the community of others in your team.

In the support chat, have your new team member share their links with you to confirm their know-how, share the team group pages, and give them all the essential info they need for day one. One of my favorite things about the support chat is that it helps people not get lost in the process. It helps make them feel comfortable and know exactly where they can come and get support.

Here are a couple of things that I like to do to keep people engaged in the support chat. You can ask them what excited them when they first tried the product and help them craft a curiosity post day one and share it. Make sure to assure them that you and the team will help validate them with commenting. Most people don't want to share because of fear of rejection or silence from friends. If they stall, it will delay their excitement, so get them into action immediately. We have a team thread where we share their link to that post so others can help them out and also get them to comment on about twenty to twenty five friends' posts before posting each time to help with their engagement. Fear of no support is what stalls most from taking action, so having a few validate their posts will help with that. Keep this chat engaged daily for at least the first week by helping them with the following steps and weekly check-ins. Don't just check in at the end of the month. Help them establish weekly goals to gather customers. Customers are the most important thing in building your business.

Love on your team and reward them, even if it is a handwritten note or gift card for coffee. Recognition is huge on social media. Most people do not even get a thank you at a job, so giving them this is very important, and it doesn't need to be just about a rank. When launching a new team member, it is important to remember that you can reward on action taken, not just sales made or rank that are hit. Find ways to include your newest team member in rewards so that they can feel like part of the community and start to look forward to what they will be a part of.

Coach's Notes: Recognition is one of the most simple acts in creating an incredible culture but can be one of the most overlooked aspects. Do NOT underestimate the value of recognition. Men die for it. Women cry for it. No matter how good you or your teams are at recognition, constantly challenge yourself to improve it. The topic of recognition is always one of the most important topics at my masterminds. We spend a good thirty minutes sharing ideas on how we can improve it.

Remember that everyone learns what to do by example. Show your team what is possible by showing up daily and being on the leaderboard yourself. If you aren't showing up daily, they are not likely to either. You need to lead by example and show your team that you are doing your own business to take care of your actions. Never stop working the business. Don't just tell them how to do this business, show them by your actions.

We are not a boss here, but we need to learn to be ok with giving direction to our team. Give your team members a task and let them return with that complete. Most people want direction and lack success in this industry because so many do not help them with the one two threes of the business. Don't keep your action steps a secret from your team. Share exactly what you did step by step to see success. That can be your own blueprint. When I started this business, I sat down and wrote out all the things I do daily on or off social media about my business, and I made that my action guide for my team to do daily. They can do it in thirty minutes to one hour daily and if they. Want results as I did? Then just rinse and repeat and do it repeatedly for hours a day.

Once your newest team member has gotten their feet wet a bit, you can have them join the team group pages for further community and support. Having guides inside your team group are key to education for your team. I set up my group for my team with guides for success. We include their getting started guide that we went over in the chat in the group and the daily action steps to take on social media. The guides are set up so that they can go through them step by step in the manner of training needed in stages to build the business. We want to make this so simple and accessible to our team that when they have a few moments a day, they can quickly locate things inside our team group to launch and grow their business.

Tag your team member on step one, day one, and move on to step two, day two, and step three, day three and then you have them in the rhythm of locating this. You want to hold their hand for two to three weeks but at the same time direct them where to locate all the things they need to build and grow. Don't continue to handhold, or you are defeating the purpose, but with the tagging and directing in the first couple of weeks, they will find their way around. People want to be shown what to do one step at a time. This helps it be easy and shows people that they can do this business!

Success is inevitable for your team if you show up and guide those who want guidance. You can't motivate others to do the work, but you can inspire them to take action through your inspired action. Eight years in this business and I can tell you one thing. This business is simple. It is simple steps repeated over and over again. Part of that process is learning how to make it simple for the newest member of your team. You are made for this! Now go out and create success.

Coach's Notes: Leonardo DaVinci says that "simplicity is the ultimate sophistication." Lori gives you the simple strategies to go through one by one to improve your duplication and get the newest person launched properly. She gives you the very basic strategies as well as advanced strategies. Use this chapter as a blueprint to get the newest person launched effectively.

LORI BENSON

Become a "NO" ADDICT!

"Hearing the word "No" is hard… I get it! However, I will tell you, the more NOs you collect, the more unstuck you will become!"

— Miss Marilyn

MISS MARILYN

- Network marketing with her company since 2013.

- Bought her starter kit as a dropout-single-mom with her last $300 while on the verge of suicide on the worst day of her life.

- With her thirteen-year-old autistic son, Maveric, at her side, she has created a powerhouse network marketing family of tens of thousands of hot pink feather boa-wearing members, The Blessed Bombshells.

- The Blessed Bombshells career sales have been over 200 million dollars in the last five years.

- Has achieved three consecutive 7-figure earning years as the first single mother to achieve this accolade.

Coach's Notes: Before you begin this powerful chapter, I want you to pay very close attention to the trials Miss Marilyn has been through. We hear cliches like the test

before the testimony or the struggle before the story but remember this. Cliches are cliches for a reason. They are timeless principles. Miss Marilyn is a powerful example that you can do and be anything you want. You either buy the excuse to fail or find the solution to succeed.

Hello! I am Miss Marilyn, and together we are going to become ADDICTS!

Your whole life, you have been taught addiction is bad...

Trust me,
I know.

I am a recovering alcoholic and drug addict. In my early twenties, I was a Magician & Fire Eater. I toured around the world performing, drinking, and doing drugs. It was a perfect time. However, it is a miracle I am still alive. I never paid for a drink or a drug. They were constantly given to me. My drug of choice was cocaine. As a child, I was consistently taught addiction was not acceptable. Yet, somehow I ended up with cocaine under my nails snorting it at the hottest clubs in Hollywood in the 90s, right along with movie stars. I could tell you so many stories of nights I was so high I didn`t think I would survive or times when my heart was racing in my chest from so many drugs I thought it would explode. But I beat my drug addiction. To this day, I find four inch straws in the hidden zipper compartment of my clutch purses from that time in my life. They constantly remind me how far I have come and how blessed I am to be still alive. Most of my friends from that era have passed away from addiction or the effects. However, I am still here. I am now all about massive success, dreaming gigantic, creating a legacy & building a life you are absolutely in love with living!

So let`s break the rules together!

Now is your time to become an addict.
But this addiction is fabulous!
Now is your time to become addicted to NO.

I want you to crave it.
I seriously want it to become your favorite word.
I want you to revel in every no.
In fact, in this chapter, we will learn to CELEBRATE the word NO!

We have always been taught it was a bad word; let`s flip that mindset together.

Network marketing is just a career where you become an expert at hearing "no."

Rejection in this industry is your best friend!
In order to become massively successful in network marketing, "No" truly needs to be your favorite word!

Oh, it`s such a glorious little word!
It can literally change your life!

Why do I love it so much?

Because every NO brings you closer to a YES!

For every 100 people you ask anything, fifteen will say yes, eighty five will say no!

Coach's Notes: This is a huge perspective. Miss Marilyn's association with no is getting closer to a yes. She embraces the no. Her mindset is a growth mindset where she focuses

on obstacles as part of the process to have success. I also love how she mentions that eighty five will say no. It is important to have perspective on what it will take to succeed in this business. Everyone wants the dream, but few are willing to EARN the dream.

So let`s get this party started!!!

WHO have you met in the past three months? Have you built relationships with them?
Have you told them about your business?

Have you gotten a "No"

Our new goal will be to get a NO from everyone we know & have met.

Look at it this way, everyone you meet is a lottery ticket & you have to scratch lottery tickets to win, right? So in this situation, we ask them a question that`s the equivalent of scratching to see if you win!

Will it be scary, yes!
Can you do it, also, yes!

Approach NOs with enthusiasm!
I was not rejected. If I don`t get fifty NOs a week at this point, I have not gone for my goals! You don`t become a 7-figure earner!

If you have ever heard me speak, you know not one single day of this business has been in my comfort zone. My family looked down on direct sales; it was never an option for me. In my early twenties, an executive from a huge company we all know called me for a meeting. I didn`t even take her seriously. It was never an option for me. I am going to be completely transparent with you; my family acted like losers do direct sales & thought it was a joke of a business. The embarrassment of being a part of it eight and a half years ago was an enormous mindset for me to conquer in my head. Although I ranked in the top five in my company in my first three months, it would take me over two years to truly embrace the thought of being in direct sales and be proud of my success from it.

I was also raised to want to hear "yes," I bet you were. Yes is nice and comfortable. It instantly puts us at ease. It is the word until now we have yearned to hear! The word "no" has been to us previously a bad thing & so was rejection. Well, you are in network marketing now & you want to be a top earner and create legacy income for your family... So let`s get rejected, and love it!

We are going to adopt my Miss Marilynaire Mindset:

No is empowering!
No is exquisite!
No is a celebration!

The more NOs you get, the more powerful you become!

Rejection will become an ADDICTION.
A fabulous lucrative addiction.
Rejection will make you brave!

We are gonna make rejection your new best friend!

Rejection will be your new strong good.

You are going to build your empire on rejection.

It`s a simple mindset shift.

After my second million in network marketing, my team started calling me Miss Marilynaire. They say I look at things differently; and rejection is a key facet of my business. No is just another word and a stepping stone to a yes! Becoming a multi-millionaire requires a tremendous amount of NOs. They have dubbed me a NO ADDICT; and that is what I want for you. For rejection to become the fuel to your fire!

I see things differently now, and I can literally watch a person work their business in a room for an hour and deduce they are afraid of no. This fear will, in all actuality, keep you broke. The goal is freedom of time and debt-free for anyone I coach. I want part of my legacy to be how I helped others create freedom in their lives. This two-letter word is vital.

The more comfortable you become with the word no &, the more you hear it, the larger your bank account will grow; and the more you can enjoy your life and help others.

It's a flip the switch mentality, meaning you have to just wake up tomorrow or right now at this moment and embrace the word "No."

Just like that, fall in love with no.

When you make $330 a day, that's $10,000 a month. How would $10,000 a month change your life?

$83,333 a month is a million dollars a year.

How would that change your life?

Let's do a dare together...
Go get your checkbook.
Write yourself a check for what you want to make monthly.

Now, how many NOs do you need?
Don't let it phase you.
You are a Badass; you can get those nos!

Do you understand the mindset shift?

We are goal-getters hunting the yes through the NOs!

The truth is I did not build my business from friends or family. To this day, not one woman in my family has bought a piece of jewelry from me. I went out and collected NOs from strangers like an addiction. This mass compilation of NOs led to the perfect yeses and a massive business that has crushed 77 million in sales in one year and over 200 million in sales since 2018. But, I put myself out there; I went and hunted NOs.

And I celebrated them!

NOs are the stepping stones to the yes and deserve a celebration! When you fully embrace this mindset, you will cash that check!

So here's another dare; I like dares better than challenges because dares are sexy!

You have a list of folks you would love on your team. I call it the "Faith List." You will start on Monday every week, and you will get twenty five NOs in seven days.

You must do this consistently as it matters.

When you don't feel like finishing the list, the question becomes, how bad do you want to cash that check. Are you willing to meet strangers and network in your community? Are you willing to grow personally? Are you willing to attend networking events?

I believe if you stay who you are, you will not cash that check.

Fear will keep you from getting your weekly NOs.
However, I believe the fear of not living your dream life should outweigh

your fear of talking to others. If I had let fear stop me, I would still be broke. I have severe fibromyalgia and a head injury. My doctors wanted me to be on disability. Although my health was unpredictable daily, I still had my brain working, and there had to be something I could do. I had a vision for my Acts Of Kindness. If I had let fear stop me, I wouldn`t have donated $20,000 to an orphanage in the Dominican Republic last year so the children could have a new kitchen. I would be stuck where I was financially eight years ago, which was poor. Not broke. I was poor. In fact, I was destitute. I had zero income; I was sick, on food stamps and Medicaid. I struggled with addiction & suicide daily. I was stuck.

Coach's Notes: The one sentence that stood out to me the most from this entire chapter was this. "I believe the fear of not living your dream life should outweigh your fear of talking to others." I would write that down and put it somewhere you can see it daily. Challenge your dreams. Challenge your FEARS. Surround yourself with an environment that helps you HIT those fears head-on! Everything worthwhile is always harder than we think it is going to be. This is a success principle. Miss Marilyn laid out the groundwork to help you embrace rejection as part of the process for SUCCESS.

I believe there is no balance; either you go all-in with your heart and soul and embrace NOs, or your life stays the same. I was destitute, as in dirt poor. My home was in foreclosure, I didn`t have a car, and I was suicidal. It was rock bottom. I found network marketing by accident, and within three months, I had a nice income. I could see the light in a pitch-black tunnel full of mind monsters. I decided to become a "no addict."

I hunt NOs. My goal is to be the best "No" hunter on the planet! Every day I strive to get NOs even after making over five million dollars in this industry in under eight years as a dropout.

MISS MARILYN

We have been taught that "no" is a bad word throughout our lifetime. We don't like hearing it. But the more NOs you hear in network marketing, the more zeros get added to your commission check! I promise you when you start paying off credit cards, your car, and your mortgage, you won't mind hearing no. You will crave it.

If you are just starting in network marketing, my best advice is to take this chapter seriously. It could be the ticket to your success! I thought I was God's practical joke. Nothing ever worked out for me. All I ever wanted was a sibling. My brother died when he was forty seven days old. I met Prince Charming, and I was engaged to get married to him when he called our wedding off just six days before it. My older son's father drowned when he was two years old. He was only twenty seven. I had my dream job at a theme park, and one day the entire park closed down. You get it; my life was filled with sorrow.

Network marketing is the only thing that has ever worked out for me. My NO addict philosophy has completely changed my life. I promise if you dare yourself to get out of your comfort zone & get addicted to NOs, you can make your dreams come true!

You may go through a lot of No's; however, that one YES makes up for all of them. I will tell you, the more NOs you get, the more unstuck you will become!

Life is short; you just gotta go for it! Do not care what anyone thinks & star in your own life!

Here's to the word "No."
May you fall in love with it!

I'll be cheering for you!
All my love,
OX
Miss Marilyn

"The credit belongs to the man who is actually in the arena; who at best knows, in the end, the triumph of high achievement, and who at the worst, if he fails, at least fails while daring greatly, so that his place shall never be with those cold and timid souls who neither know victory nor defeat."

— Theodore Roosevelt (1910)

MORGAN ZAMBRANO

- Joined Network Marketing in 2017.

- Company Car Earner 2018.

- Verified Six-Figure Earner 2020.

- Go Pro Speak Off Winner 2020.

- Featured Panelist of Most Powerful Women in Network Marketing 2022.

Coach's Notes: This chapter is one of the most important topics in all of network marketing. TIME and how you use it. We all have the exact same amount of time each day but mastering how one uses that time is vital. I want you to think about this thought. On average, billionaires don't work harder than millionaires. On average, millionaires don't work harder than those who make six figures annually. Lastly, think about this one. There

are many people who make minimum wage who work more hours than the successful. Now, of course, each person and situation is different. I am only illustrating the point that time is the most valuable thing we have on this earth. To be more successful, we all must learn how to LEVERAGE time properly. Morgan can teach you because she has done it.

Be honest. Do you ever wonder if you have enough time to build your business successfully?

Between full-time jobs, children, spouses, chores, errands, having hobbies, staying healthy, and maintaining friendships...can you really run a successful business too?

When I joined network marketing in 2017, I wondered the same thing. At the time, I had a 6 month old baby, a wild 4-year-old, I was working full time in a stressful career, and my husband was working nights. I would come home at 6 pm, emotionally exhausted from my day, kiss my husband goodbye for his shift at 7 pm, and take care of my children alone in the evenings. Weekends were usually a juggle of my husband and I picking up extra shifts and overtime, trying to dig out of living paycheck to paycheck.

We had no time. No time to be together. No time to be a family. No time for ourselves. I knew this wasn't what it was supposed to look like, but it felt like there was no other way. That's why I was desperate to find a way. I didn't want my husband to work nights for the extra two dollars an hour. I didn't want to miss my baby's milestones while he took his first steps at daycare. I didn't want to say no to field trips or have to scramble on sick days. If you currently have no time to spare... how does that make you feel?

At the beginning of building my business, I learned how to make time by staying up later to work on the content and waking up earlier to do live videos. I learned to prioritize time by skipping the late-night social media scroll and turning it into income-producing activities. Most importantly, I learned to utilize tiny pockets of time, finding five minutes here and there. Even today, I`m currently writing this at 11 pm. My kids are asleep, my husband is asleep, and do not disturb is on my phone. It`s just me and my laptop.

I have been a full-time network marketer for multiple years, and this is still when I do my best work. Would you be willing to sacrifice small pockets of time, replace your Netflix binging, and wake up a little earlier if it means building the life of your dreams? I will break down a few of my favorite strategies for maximizing your time and building your business into any schedule.

First, we are going to do an activity. Take a piece of paper, and write down ALL of your business tasks. I know that`s a big assignment, but write down as many as you can.

You might write things like using my products, share my products with others, share my story, go live, post on social media, follow up with customers, send an email campaign, etc. You can be as detailed as you would like.

Next, I would like you to write down how long you think each task takes. If you wrote down "live video," this could take anywhere from two minutes to two hours. Maybe you do fifteen minutes of follow-up a day. Posting on social media five to ten minutes. This list doesn`t have to be perfect. It will be enough to get you started.

You are not only building a list of your business activities, but now you are going to understand how you can puzzle piece them into your day. The next time you find yourself with five minutes, you know what tasks you can fit within that time frame. You can immediately take action when you have ten minutes, two minutes, etc.

Coach's Notes: This simple strategy is a game-changer. We are used to having bosses telling us what to do and when to do it. Even still, it is so challenging to stay focused. When you have a list of tasks and how long they should take, you begin to create a next-level focus. Remember now that you don't have the typical boss. Your new boss is your calendar/schedule or, as they say in the UK for the calendar, your diary.

The strategy might sound "too" simple. It isn't. The problem is we overthink, and instead of sending 5 minutes of messages, we spend five minutes worrying about what people will think if we message them. We overthink ourselves out of taking action and spend most of our work time spinning wheels in our minds instead of doing the work.

I have an "execution problem." This is where I used to get stuck. I had all the information I needed, I even knew what to do, but something was holding me back. I could think of all the big ideas, sit all day, and learn, but my to-do list haunted me at the end of the day. Maybe it was overwhelming; maybe it was a lack of confidence or a lack of belief that it would work for me. But whatever the reasoning was, I knew I had all of the information at my fingertips if I could get myself to see the path for how to get it all done. Maybe you feel that way about this book. You have all the answers right here, but will you put them into action?

Or, maybe you feel the opposite. Instead of having an execution problem, you feel like you are constantly working, learning, and implementing. You never stop taking action, and for some reason, nothing is creating the results you desire.

Have you ever started doing the dishes and then decided to walk around your house just in case your kids left out a cup or bowl? Then while walking around, you trip on a toy, so you start picking up the toys. As you're picking up the toys, you figure you might as well start a load of laundry. Then you have to pick up your kids from school, then it's dinner, then bedtime, and suddenly it's the end of the day, and you didn't finish the dishes, you didn't pick up the toys, and the clothes are still in the washer. You feel like you were busy all day but haven't accomplished anything.

This is how it felt working in my business. I would sit down to work on one activity, then jump to another activity, then get a message, then a notification, I'd get lost scrolling on Facebook, then suddenly it's the end of the day, and I can't think of anything I finished!

I was busy all the time, but I wasn't getting anything done!

Distraction is one of the biggest pitfalls in our efficiency. Distraction comes cloaked, and disguised as work. It's the message you think you need to answer now. It's the to-do list that all feels equally important. It's priding yourself on being a "multi-tasker" instead of being able to focus & complete.

Remember your list of business activities? It's time to bring out your list again. When I learned how to take my business activities and turn them into power hours based on the time frame of each activity, something immediately shifted.

We call them "Power Hours," and they changed the game. No longer was I jumping from one activity to another. No longer was every message or notification taking away from my current projects. I learned how to maximize my time on each activity by focusing on one activity for specified amounts of time.

For someone used to multi-tasking, this can be the opposite of being productive. When you are used to attempting three tasks at once, learning to focus on one at a time feels like a step backward. I challenge you to try it for one week. Just one hour a day. Build your perfect hour, and then grab a timer.

How many messages can you send in five minutes? How many comments can you make in ten? Can you get skilled enough to send an email campaign in six minutes?

It will almost become a game. Can you do more work tomorrow than you did today? Can you squeeze in one last message in the last ten seconds? Can you do it with a friend and see who can prospect the most people in a short time frame?

There are two rules to a power hour:

1. You MUST keep track of your activities. If you are sending messages; how many did you send? How many comments did you make?

2. You can ONLY do that activity. No responding to messages. No checking notifications. No scrolling or squirreling. Laser focus on that one activity until the timer goes off.

You will quickly learn which activities you love and which can be removed. You'll figure out which activities aren't worth the time and you should double the amount of time on.

You will quickly learn your most efficient activities by doing a structured power hour daily.

You probably have way more activities on your list than you can do in an hour, and you might wonder where to start. One of the most important lessons I can teach you is just to start. A good friend once told me, that you can do anything for five minutes; just begin and see what happens. You may have an activity for five minutes that takes ten, or an activity for fifteen that you find you can do in three. You will consistently tweak your power hour until you find the perfect for you, so pick a starting point and know it will change daily!

Here are ideas to get you started!

- Ten minutes commenting on friend's social media posts
- Ten minutes commenting in hobby groups
- Ten minutes adding new friends
- Ten minutes messaging follow-ups
- Ten minutes messaging to say hi
- Ten minutes messaging to book parties
- Ten minutes messaging the opportunity
- Ten minutes messaging downlines
- Ten minutes planning out your next week's content
- Three minutes to message all birthdays
- Ten minutes batching stories
- Two-minute break, write down one goal for next week

You might say, "Morgan, this is all great, but I don't even have an hour." Do you have ten minutes? Five minutes? two minutes? Because if you start taking five minutes of action every time you used to let it pass by, that five minutes will make a difference.

You have your business activities, your time frames, and your timer. You have the resources to make those five minutes actionable. Suddenly five minutes isn't five minutes. five minutes is five messages. five minutes is ten comments. Five minutes is sharing your product.

When comparing two network marketers at the same level in business, one says, "I only have five minutes," and one says, "in five minutes, I know I can message five people." One will have five minutes plus five minutes plus five minutes added up to hours of wasted time, and one has five minutes plus five minutes plus five minutes added up to massive action. Who do you think is going to get farther faster? Your results will compound over time. Your skills will get better; you will get more confident and faster.

What if the difference in your long-term results is simply reframing how you look at your time?

Coach's Notes: The power hour is an absolute must if you want to hit the top ranks. Your version may be different, but I love how specific Morgan is because it gives you a vision of what it takes. You may decide that forty five minutes is good or two different thirty minutes sessions a day. The main point is to start and then improve your version of pour hour to hyper-focus on crushing your business.

MORGAN ZAMBRANO

"Always have the 'Courage to Love' on everyone you meet."

— Randy Christopher

RANDY CHRISTOPHER

- Started network marketing in 2013.

- Planted feet in the current company on August 21st, 2014.

- Rose six ranks in first six months with current company.

- Hosts annual event every single year for team and company for eight consecutive years.

- Rose to the top earner`s group.

Being successful at anything in life requires two key things: commitment and consistency. Just reading those two words will bring up many questions for yourself. What do consistency and commitment mean to you? When asked, an individual may say "commitment means finishing what has been started," but another may say "it means setting goals and completing them." Let me stop you right there. When discussing goals, if you are setting goals that you`re meeting every month, those are not goals. You have made a bunch of tasks given that you know you will accomplish them before you set them. Let's dig a little deeper into the definition of commitment.

Coach's Notes: I am glad Randy took on this topic. Commitment is a bad word to many. It is a scary word, but it is also one of the most important aspects of achieving success. If you can't keep your commitments, not only will others not trust you, but you won't trust yourself. If you can't trust yourself, you will constantly self-sabotage your business. Randy will break down the different aspects of commitment to help you start small and scale your business big time.

Think about someone that is on your network marketing team, and they set a goal to re-rank every month for the next six months and easily make it each and every month. While some consider this a goal, it has now become a task easily accomplished every month. You have to set goals that help you look forward to your future and push you to become the next best version of yourself and begin a new chapter. You need to think of numbers that will scare you as your goal. Think of it this way, find a number or rank, then double it. Now you have a goal that top earners of your company pushed for. Be committed to hitting these goals no matter what!

This is what commitment looks like. Taking each day and setting yourself up for success. Those goals are a marker that is virtually impossible to reach. It may take until midnight on closeout nights to reach. You may not reach your goal that month. However, that is okay; yes, that is okay if you miss that major goal. Look how much further you got by pushing for a goal rather than achieving tasks. Now pick yourself up, dust yourself off, reset that goal, figure out why you did not reach that goal, and start again. I haven't hit my goals in this industry many times. That doesn't mean I have failed; I have learned and gotten the experiences that will set me up for future successes.

Look how much you have achieved while you were staying committed and consistent when going after the goal. Part of staying committed to your goal is saying what you will do and implementing it. Have you ever noticed how it is easier to show up when you are committed to showing up for someone else? We will show up at the gym and work out if we know our friend is waiting on us. But if we have to go to the gym by ourselves, so many people don't do it. Why is that? This has to do with not respecting ourselves enough to show up and do what we say we will, even when no one else is watching.

I see so many people get their feelings hurt when they don't reach their goals. Remember, it is not always about that set goal, and it is about staying committed and consistent with the goal and yourself. Commitment isn't easy, and it is not supposed to be. Most of the time, commitment is challenging when we are at our weakest. When you are learning to be committed to your business, you may need help being accountable. Ask for help! Accountability partners can be perfect for many different reasons. One example is when a leader sees a meeting coming up, they will post about it, call people who are in their downline, set up rooms at or near the meeting, and consistently check in to offer ideas of how and what to do to get to the meeting. They act as that accountability partner for you. Let's dig deeper into what consistency means.

What does consistency look like in network marketing? I tell them that consistency is striving to finish what you have started, no matter how long it takes. You don't hit your goals in a day. To accomplish the goal, it may take working hard, going all-in day after day, night after night, sometimes week after week, month after month. Goals take time and require you to show up in the good, the bad, and the ugly of life.

Push to stay consistent in your network marketing business even after your "task(s)" are completed. I've seen some people hit their "task" numbers by the middle of the month. Instead of staying consistent, they will say they are just going to coast for the rest of the month. If your stop being consistent all month long, you start creating a pattern with yourself of meeting a task and quitting when the task becomes smaller or more straightforward. Taking less time causes your commitment to slack which causes your business to down spiral. You will see that your business can grow so much faster by staying consistent all month long.

One great tool to help you become consistent in your business is a Daily Method of Operation (DMO). These are tasks you set yourself to do every day to help move your business forward. Your DMO should fit what works best for you in your life daily. If you're being consistent with your DMO, you will have success. You may need to tweak your DMO so it works for you in the best way possible. You can have more than one DMO in your life. For example, I have DMOs around building my organization, for being a leader and checking in with my downline, and even for things to do around the house.

DMOs are not a mandatory thing that someone can tell you to do or how it should look; it is for you to put together, so it fits your particular lifestyle. Your mentor can help teach you what it could look like and give you an example. But you have to turn around with that information and make that DMO. One that will work for you. Finding the perfect DMO for yourself will help you stay committed and consistent.

Coach's Notes: In the traditional job world, we are told what to do and when to do it. We are given expectations and deadlines to meet. This gives us focus. In network marketing is exciting knowing that you can do what you want when you want, but with that

benefit comes a huge danger. We tend to procrastinate on everything. We tend to lose discipline and focus. Nothing becomes urgent. Creating your own DMO, as Randy said, is CRITICAL to success. Discipline isn't to take away from everything you ever wanted. Discipline is instead there to give you everything you ever wanted. You are your boss now, but the real boss is your schedule. Create that DMO and focus on it!

Helping others be committed; Committed and consistent

In network marketing, we have the opportunity to help other people become the best versions of themselves. When we start in this business, we may be learning how to do things differently than we ever have before. This means you will be helping many people learn how to be committed to their goals and stay consistent.

Part of your DMO could be an encouragement, letting the newest people in your business know, "I believe in you. I trust you. I know you are going to do great things". They consider you their mentor, and you need to show up that way. Encouraging your team to build goals and checking in on them to see how they are helping teach consistency and commitment through duplication, you`re teaching them through your actions. When you teach duplication, you are teaching consistency. I know this to be true! You may have heard this phrase before "your team will do what you do." If you`re not consistent with what your doing, your team will not be consistent either. Make sure to be the example of consistency.

Consistency and duplication are not about being precise. It is about duplicating the principle. Not everybody is the same, and everyone has different learning abilities and ways of approaching things. It will be up to you to see how you can teach commitment and consistency as a principle without making it precise. It would be impossible for me to jump on a call with each team member every day to see if they are keeping their commitments. But as the team has grown with amazing leaders, I have seen the system that we put in place have duplicated and is being taught to others. This has created such an amazingly supportive community and strong culture on our team.

I love the company culture that I partnered with because the owners are great examples of being committed and consistent. The company owners take the time out of their life to jump on calls with teams and encourages people, and teaches them as well. That is such a great example to me and other leaders about what it looks like to stay consistent and duplicate that. We should always show our team what commitment looks like from the top down. Often, top leaders will vacate, leaving their newest people stranded. Remember, what you do in your business duplicates in your team. A great way to help people learn principles is to always be an example of commitment. This also gives them the freedom to make adjustments and find what will work best for them. Being a successful leader is all about knowing when to lead, mentor, and follow, as Rob Sperry mentioned in his book, *Your Rank Advancement Blueprint*.

How to stay committed and consistent during hard times

Life happens, and we all have emergencies and curveballs come up in our lives. So how do you stay committed and consistent during those times? First, decide what an emergency is. Too often, we drop our commitments because we are too tired, too overwhelmed, or don't believe we will ever accomplish it. Don't quit during these times, and remember that you are building an empire. You are building your future, and don't quit because you are tired. We all have to look deep down in our hearts and not let things stop us, even if it is challenging.

I see things like being tired, unmotivated, or fearful as enemies, not emergencies. We have to decide which version of ourselves we want to be. Find the commitments that you want to be completely committed to. It can be your family, business, or friends.

Success is available for anyone in network marketing. That is one of the reasons I love this industry. But you need to remember that everyone has different timing. Want to know how to make success inevitable? Stay committed and consistent. Think about two people in a marathon, one person may start sprinting, and the other may start with a slow-paced jog. The person that is sprinting may get tired, lose focus, and quit. But the person that stays consistent and committed in their slower-paced build will eventually reach the finish line.

Sometimes the hard times aren`t necessarily hard times, but maybe it is hard people in our lives. Not everyone has a supportive community of people around them when they start network marketing. We have to remember that commitment and consistency aren`t something that other people do for us. We are the only ones that can do it for ourselves. Please don`t let people with small vision and perspective keep you from achieving your dreams. I remember someone on my team telling me about a person in their town. They went to the same high school, and this person was still acting as the school bully. She was talking sarcastically about network marketing, and it got to my team member. I told her, "It`s not her job to understand your dream. That is your job". I reminded her that she wasn`t in high school anymore, and she didn`t have to shoot off something equally sarcastic and rude. I told her to smile and come back with wins in her business; that would be the ultimate win. She did just that, and the key was to not get in the weeds of other people`s drama and stay consistent with your own life. Don`t let other people make your vision blurry.

Conclusion

One of the best things that I get to see is people be so successful in network marketing that they get to walk away from their nine to five jobs, that never gets old to me. I have seen stay-at-home moms make enough money to bring home their husbands. I have shed countless tears in persona and on the phone hearing people making their dreams come true. That isn't something that just happens to me; there is no greater success than to be able to help people create an empire that supports the family. I pray daily that I find people that are willing to commit and stay consistent with their dreams. People need you. They need you to show up and be willing to do the work first so that they can follow your lead and see what that looks like. Be strong, believe in yourself, put in the time, and watch your commitment and consistency grow. Your family will flourish when you show up as the best version of yourself.

Each and every one of you is building an empire for your family, never forget that! No matter what happens in your life. No matter what happens in this business, stay laser-focused on building an empire for your family. All of this depends on the critical factors of commitment and consistency. Without those two things, you're never going to be the successful person that you want to be, whether it's in everyday life or your network marketing business. Let God prevail in your life by being committed and consistent with your dreams and desires.

Coach's Notes: Your level of commitment will largely determine your level of success. Can you do this business? YES! Is it worth it? YES! It may take you longer than you expected, but if you are genuinely committed, I believe the network marketing profession is too good for you not to achieve success. When you are committed, your brain will begin to focus on solutions rather than problems. This is when you begin to think and act on an entirely new level!

RANDY CHRISTOPHER

"First, it is an intention. Then a behavior. Then a habit. Then a practice. Then second nature. Then it is simply who you are."

— Brendon Burchard

RHONDA ARZA

- Was a full-time horse trainer and riding instructor for twenty eight years before she began her Network Marketing career.

- She has been in the Network Marketing space for six years.

- In her most recent company, she built to the top rank in her company in 5 months and created seven 6-figure income earners in her downline in one year.

- She leads a team of over 2,000 distributors.

- In her first two years in business, she generated over 8 million in team sales.

I homeschooled our incredibly talented, smart, wise beyond his years, "differently-abled" son from the time he was ten through high school. His unique learning style taught me that in order to get the best from him, build his confidence, and teach him that his remarkable way of thinking was his incredible gift, I had to understand how to draw and focus on his strengths rather than focus on what he wasn't good at. Of course, we worked on those things, but our main focus was to help him grow his strengths and allow his out-of-the-box thinking to be his genius path and lead him to a successful life ahead that, as an adult, he now enjoys.

This philosophy that came naturally to me as his teacher became my leadership strength and taught me to draw greatness from the people I bring into my network marketing business.

I am an observer of human nature, and I have seen many incredible leadership styles work so well for different people in my organization and in others. By understanding what makes people tick, and especially what makes you tick, you will find your own particular gift and find this in others.

I have found three basic types of leaders in our industry in my observations. They are: teachers, sales stars, and recruiters. Don't get me wrong many have mastered all three and have been able to take what was once a weakness and make it their biggest strength. But initially, when a person is starting out, I find it most beneficial to build on what they are best at and teach them to find the other paths within that initial strength. I will tell you what each leader is, which can help you identify your strength to build on them.

Coach's Notes: I have personally worked with Rhonda the last year. I love that it is so incredible to understand each person has different gifts. Just think of sports. Can you imagine if every coach tried to make every basketball player the point guard with no other positions? Can you imagine in baseball if the coach tried to make everyone the pitcher with no other focus on other positions? To create a great team, you want to

identify each person's unique strength and focus on it. This is one of those rare topics in network marketing that is seldom spoken about.

First, we have our teachers. They tend to like to lead large groups, bring information that is helpful to the table, and teach everything they learn. The teacher feels most fulfilled when they are learning and adding value. They are in this to serve, and as long as they feel they are serving enough people, they are happy.

Next, we have our sales stars. This group can sell the heck out of the product. They are so great at selling that no one can even figure out what they are saying or how they are even doing it. They have this "IT" factor that attracts everyone to their product. They know what to say and how to say it. They love the product, and they live to sell it to everyone and anyone within arm`s length of them.

Coach's Notes: Doesn't this information help?! I am guessing you are now thinking of several people on your team and their personalities. I would take a moment to assess their style and how you can best serve them. I would take a moment to start to assess how you can help them double down on their unique strengths. As your organization grows, this chapter will become more and more critical in your journey to hit the highest ranks.

The final of the three is our recruiters. They are all about the business. Most in this group have no interest in the details of the product, the comp plan, or anything in between. They don`t understand any of it or have the need to as it slows them down. They love the thrill of the victory of bringing new people to the table. The more people they can get in front of, and the faster the pace, the better for this group.

As you can imagine, being all three of these or even two of them would be of great value to a team. Those, to me, are the true unicorns of the business. But if you are a smart leader, you will be able to partner with each of these and allow them to do what they do the best, expand upon it, and even pick up the slack. This, to me, is the ultimate partnership and what working as a team is all about.

For example, if you have a great recruiter who comes in on fire, you do NOT want to slow them down. You can NOT tell a recruiter to go and learn the comp plan or get more product knowledge because they will die on the vine. Instead, you need to say, "Listen, Susie, your recruiting skills are incredible. I can handle your new recruits. All you need to do is plug them into me and my system and continue doing what you do best."

A great recruiter will feel so much relief if they have a supportive leader who can keep it simple for them and allow them to soar.

If you have someone who is an excellent teacher, point out to them that building community and teams will be the thing that will keep them going. Allow them space within your organization to grow and teach while encouraging them to build. Helping them understand that they aren`t serving enough people if they don`t feel fulfilled. The more people they can serve, the more they will create a platform for learning for others. A great teacher can build gigantic teams once they find their stride and realize their positive influence on others. Give them the platform, and watch them soar. These people are true community builders and will create a culture of growth and learning far beyond the product or the comp plan. Great teachers can be the biggest rock stars in a business when permitted to soar in this space.

Unicorn salespeople truly have passion for the products they sell. So much so that they forget that offering the business to others is a gigantic opportunity for them. They tend to have another interest that is heavily aligned with the product and may even view business builders as competitors. They are so good at making the product a part of what they do on a daily basis that they forget to offer the business as a viable option to their customers. They are very gifted at sales, people like them, they are charismatic, and people see them as great influencers.

The question is, how do you help each type stay in their lane of genius while also building upon what they are great at?

Sales stars

1. Teach them the magic question:

    When they go to close a sale, they need to always ask, "Would you like to purchase as a customer or as a distributor." This will help them lead with the business and overcome objections.

2. Use their sales gift to build their distributor's customer base.

    They need to explain that they are great at sales, it's true, but that's the beauty of working as a team. The only thing their new people have to do is connect them. They will learn the skills and have the support of the sales star to help close their sales, making them more duplicatable.

3. Live in the abundance mindset that fewer customers and more distributors are much more sustainable long term. They can always sell, but selling the business will create a much larger long-term residual income for them.

Recruiters

1. Teach them to enjoy selling the product to those who said no to the business but yes to it by creating a referral program with their customers. In essence, it's like having a new recruit because, in essence, they are asking their customers to be their best referrers.

2. Make sure they do their part with their new recruit by helping them close their recruits. They can also be great at three-way validations and duplication if they are good at recruiting.

3. Make sure they know the basics of the system you have in place so that their new recruits don't get lost in the shuffle of their quick process. They move on to the next so quickly, they need to understand how to step by step get someone started without slowing them down at all.

Teachers

1. Allow them to lead your team, go live, and do weekly trainings.

2. Help them build on their own recruiting skills because if they recruit quickly enough and create their own community, they will rise quickly to the top of your organization.

3. Mentoring one-on-one with a great teacher will be worth your effort. The teacher type will always make the best future leader, and they will always appreciate the guidance.

As you look through these three types of individuals, I'm sure you see yourself in one or more of them. I was certainly a teacher/recruiter type, but my personal product sales skills weren't a strength, so I had to work on my mindset around it.

I learned that if I could teach my customers to be the best at referring their network, I could satisfy my love of recruiting and teaching because essentially I was able to teach my customers to be like team members. It was a huge aha moment for me, and when I have a great recruiter, I always teach them to recruit their customers the same way. It satisfies their desire to recruit and often bridges the gap between retailing and recruiting by marrying the two and opening up the conversation for transitioning customers to distributors.

For you, it will be important to recognize where you are in this process to look for people with other strengths than you have. This will create a literal dream team of talent in your downline. Imagine your organization with so many fantastic leaders who possess one or more of these strengths... Imagine how much you can co-create!

I challenge myself to bring out the best in myself and work on what I am not as strong at, but I do not expect a zebra to change its stripes. Understand the only person you can truly change is yourself, so complaining that Susie isn't a great recruiter but can sell the heck out of the product won't help you or Susie. Instead, you need to show Suzie how simple it is to lead with the business, and selling the business is precisely the same as selling the product. You just have to listen a little bit longer so you can fill both needs simultaneously. This is a huge aha moment for the rock star salesperson and will change them for good.

When I first started with my current company, I had a coach who pointed out that I was born to serve and teach, and the only reason I was not feeling fulfilled in my life was that I wasn't serving enough people. She told me that my vision was stuck within looking for followers rather than finding other leaders who could be empowered through my ability to pinpoint their strengths and then doing my part to fill in the gaps so they could soar.

This was when everything came together very quickly for me, and I stopped trying to change others and recognized it was identical to what I did for my son while we homeschooled. I had to bring out the very best in each individual and draw from what they do well to get the most out of them. The simple systems I created resulted in duplication for each type of individual. As a team we have grown a beautiful organization filled with Teachers, Sales Stars, and Recruiters that all work synergistically to create one fantastic dream team. Our team's goal is to make a difference in the lives of others while bringing out the very best in each other. I wish that type of ease and flow for every team out there created in this amazing space that we are all so blessed to be a part of.

Coach's Notes: Stephen Covey always used to say, "begin with the end in mind." If you are new, this chapter will give you a vision of the different types of team members. If you have a large organization, this will be a training that you will want to study repeatedly to help you best maximize the team. Everything rises and falls on leadership. A big part of leadership is the ability to empower others in their unique talents. Regardless of how much success you have had, you can still empower others to become the best version of themselves.

RHONDA ARZA

"Do the thing you fear to do and keep on doing it…that is the quickest and surest way ever yet discovered to conquer fear."

– Dale Carnegie

SANDY HUMPEL

- The first person in her family to earn a million dollars and become debt-free by the age of forty.

- Paying cash for kid`s colleges (no student loans for them).

- Top earner in the company in first eighteen months.

- Helped 100 people so far become six-figure earners and helped even more, retire from their nine to five job.

- Earned over twenty lavish paid for vacations.

Coach's Notes: FEAR! Ahh, I love any chapter or book that focuses on this aspect because I believe mindset will eat skills and systems for breakfast. If you can't learn to hit your fears head, it won't even matter how great your skills become. You will become the broke know it if you can't learn to deal with your fears. Learn from Sandy how to deal with them and how to

teach dealing with them. Then go grab my book, *The Game of Conquering.*

Have you ever heard the saying, "feel the fear and do it anyway"?

I was living in fear and doing it anyway ten years ago. As a stay-at-home mom, I was feeling completely lost with no direction. I felt like everyone else around me had it all figured out, but I just couldn't seem to get it together or figure out what I wanted. It felt like life was happening to me all of the time. I was a high school dropout teen mom with zero college education and very little life experience. It felt like I was still trying to decide who I would be when I grew up. Have you ever been there? Feeling like your life looks completely different than other people around you? Have you ever felt like everyone else has it figured out, and you are behind the curve? It never feels good. It never feels good to think that you are lost and wandering, no matter what circumstances you are going through.

I think that is one of my favorite parts of this industry. It doesn't matter who you are, where you come from, and your present circumstances. You can start network marketing exactly where you are at right now. Network marketing was dropped into my lap. I was so terrified when I started that I laughed that someone would want to sign me up. I had never run a business before; I was terrified, thinking about being online and wondering if anyone would want to buy anything from me. It felt like maybe I was signing up for one more thing that I would fail at, just like everything else in my life at that time.

Fear of the unknown stops so many of us from even signing up. We start to believe the stories spinning around in our heads or the stories that are being told to us by other people. We start to question everything, and we start to fight for our limitations. Please don't believe your own negative self-talk or that negative self-talk being told to you. It is not true! But I can see how easy it is to get stuck in the cycle of self-doubt. I see you! I can see some of you reading this book right now and thinking about all of the unknowns of doing this business. Stop right now and listen to me. It`s ok to feel the fear and do it anyway. The moment I signed up, all of the fear started coming up about everything. But, at that moment, I made a choice. I decided that it was time for me to face my fear and go after it anyway.

Coach's Notes: Think about this. I am so grateful we have doctors but let's put it in perspective. Doctors go to school for twelve plus years. They come out of school with massive amounts of debt. Most doctors don't make as much money as you think (they still do well) especially when they are just starting out. It takes them years and years after the twelve years of school to climb out of debt. Why are they willing to do this? For starters, it may be a passion, but the bigger perspective is that the fear of the unknown is gone. They have a set career path. It is clear how long it will take them to make x amount. In network marketing because we don't know when or even if it will happen we begin to panic. Marry the process and divorce the results. If you stick with network marketing working your business deliberately and consistently I believe you have incredible odds of having success.

I wanted to be different. I wanted to learn how to show up for myself and my life. I started to use fear as my driving force; I wanted to learn how to master fear and conquer fears. For any of you that are in this same place, I want to encourage you to show up for yourself. It can be a moment. But face the fear and show up. Fear is an interesting thing. It has so many people stuck, and what I want to show you is that it doesn`t take huge action to get over the fear, it takes consistency.

It wasn't some explosive change at first. It was hard to see myself as a businesswoman that could financially take care of my family. I knew if I couldn't see myself there, I could borrow my hope and wish from other people. I started to find stories of other women. I wanted to learn their stories, backgrounds, education, and experience. I wanted to see myself in their stories and believe that if they could make it happen, there was a chance that I could too. I learned of thousands of women who had similar backgrounds, who had found success in this industry, and had admitted they had the same fears as myself. The more stories I read and saw examples of, the more I would think, "This could work for me." It's ok to borrow confidence and success from other people in the beginning. I want to encourage you to find other people that are like you. Seek out stories that bring you hope and encouragement that you can use as examples.

When I was able to find other women like myself, I was able to say, "LOOK at them. They overcame obstacles like my own and became a success."

What I learned about fear was for me, it worked to start with small fears; I started to jot down when something made me feel anxious, nervous, or scared and put it on my weekly to-do list. some big fears for me were speaking to a crowd, asking if people were interested, etc. Fear became a challenge, almost like a game for me against me. I set out to get over my fears with tears in my eyes, a shaky voice, and weak knees.

I'll never forget the first time I was asked to speak to 1,000 people, and I agreed and wanted to crawl into a hole. I was so scared; I didn't look perfect like the others; I had only been in the industry a few years and didn't have the experience others had. I suffered from staying on topic, if you haven't noticed yet, and low and behold, my greatest fear came true. I was backstage with all of the top earners, pacing the floors, and suddenly my entry song came on, and it was my turn to walk onto the most significant stage I had seen in my life. I walked onto the stage with trembling legs and sweaty armpits. Suddenly, the music stopped, and it was time for me to begin my training/message to the audience. Everything was silent, and my thoughts were empty; I had forgotten everything I had stressed and worked hard on for weeks. SO I had forgotten everything, what I was shaking, what I thought I would die. I laughed when I wanted to cry. I began to joke and make fun of myself and then began to turn the message into just this. My message became clear, if we do not act on our fears without the worry of judgment or failure, we will never overcome our fears.

Coach's Notes: One of the most powerful paragraphs that I want you to read again is this. "What I learned about fear was for me, it worked to start with small fears; I started to jot down when something made me feel anxious, nervous, or scared and put it on my weekly to-do list; some big fears for me were speaking to a crowd, asking if people were interested, etc. Fear became a challenge, almost like a game for me against me. I set out to get over my fears with tears in my eyes, a shaky voice, and weak knees."

Sandy started small. She even created a checklist. Sandy is a big leader who had massive fears but she found small and simple ways to focus on progress. YOU CAN DO THIS!!!!

"Happy, Healthy, Wealthy is the way to be!"

— My quote for years

SONIA LINE ARSENEAU

- Top twenty ranked leaders.

- Inducted into 7 figure earner hall of fame in 2020.

- Recruited over 500 people.

- Created her own maternity leave for her second kid.

- Retired her husband and home/unschooling her kids.

- Joined as a founding member and didn`t quit when it got tough.

Plan, Do, Review

Before I even got into this company, I was working on my happiness by doing new habits like gardening, taking walks in nature, hugging trees, and spending time with my family and my pets. As I started to feel better myself, I started looking into other things I could do to improve my health and wellness. I was introduced to the company, and the products really helped me. I loved how each time I worked on improving an area of my life, I got even better at having my own back and learning what else I could improve. Once I began feeling great with the new products I was using, I started working on my wealth. I share all of this with you because this was the system that worked for me. I know I wouldn't have been successful if I had started with every single area in my life. Systems are so important because as we start to use them, we see how they can work for us.

I am excited to share with you one of the greatest things I have done in my network marketing business to create success. I know that I have been successful because of the systems that I have consistently stuck to. I want to teach you why systems are beneficial and how to stick to them. I chose this topic mainly because it is something that I am always working on and it keeps me balanced.

One of my mentors says, "plan, do, review." This is the most straightforward way to define what a system is. Simply put, a system is something that is planned out that you can follow. It is a step-by-step guide done for you.

Next, a system only works if you do it! Finally, you need to review what you did. How did the system work? What results did you create for yourself? What needs to be tweaked?

I have been with the same company since 2014, and I wish I would have implemented this earlier. This was a brand new company when I started. My upline left after not even two months in the business, so I was left to do everything on my own. I was learning this business in my second language with a company in a different country than I was. Some of you may be in this exact situation. It can be intimidating to feel like you are supposed to lead people when you're still trying to figure it out!

Most of our lives have been run on systems. None of us wake up in the morning and wonder what we will do. We all have a morning system that we do. Perhaps you do meditation, prayer, or reading in the morning. That would be part of your system. Whether you believe that you follow them or not, we all have natural systems and schedules that we follow in our lives. When you go shopping for food, you have a system of making your way through the store. When you take a vacation, you have a system of how you pack items in your luggage and even a system for what items you will bring.

Coach's Notes: "Most of our lives have been run on systems." So true. For most of us, it is groundhog day every single week. We wake up at similar times. We eat similar things. We drink similar things. We get off work at similar times. Show me your habits, and I will show you your future. Systems will help set you up for success.

Everyone has a different way of living their lives. If we all compared our mornings, they would be very different. So why do we think we need to build businesses the same way as everyone else? When people first start network marketing, they think there is only one way to be successful. Maybe you are brand new to network marketing, or maybe you are restarting or relaunching your business. It doesn't matter where you are at; you will want to find the systems that work best for you that help you save time and money and lessen the frustration you may face.

Systems can also help build your business by helping customers and future business partners. Think about how your customers purchase products. What is the system you have in place that helps them? What about follow-up so that you can ensure they are getting the support they need? Think about your journey into network marketing. How did you start in the business? Were you a customer? Did you start as an affiliate? How did a system help you go from where you started to where you are today in the industry?

If you are like most people who start network marketing, you will want to be as efficient as you can with your time. That includes using systems that will help you answer questions, get people signed up, and do other tasks to ensure everyone gets the same info and chance and can easily duplicate. As a business builder in network marketing, systems also help you cut through wasting time on the same situation repeatedly.

Three types of systems

I like to break my systems down into three different areas: business, customer, and personal. Here are a couple of ideas for each area. Let's start with the business. When someone joins your business, what do you do? How do you get that person the information they need? How do you add them as part of a community? How do you check-in and help support them as they learn the business? All of these questions can be solved by a system. I like to have a business system in place that has the next step of exactly what action I need to take and the timeline. For example, my system might be to send a congratulations email twenty four hours after someone enrolls. Send a text message with the first steps to join the Facebook group twenty four hours after the email, etc.

Hopefully, you and the person who just joined will create a really great relationship because of the environment that you help create for them to join. Don't start the relationship on the wrong foot by dropping the ball with your systems.

The main thing is that you want to create systems that you can easily follow. When you set up your systems, I highly recommend that you start to write them down. You can use a success guide, an action planner, or even a blank document on your computer. Depending on your company, they may even supply you with some of their easy-to-use systems that you can start with, and then as you use them, start to make them your own.

Next, know your market and customer base. For example, there are so many possibilities to incorporate into your life. I am in a little village where there are about 1,200 people. The next village over has a hundred. There is one gas station in this area. I know what people are interested in. I know what products and services will be great sellers. As you build your business, listen to your markets.

Finally, work on your system that will help you improve yourself and take care of your own needs as you work on your business. Self-development is always huge for me. I like to read/listen to ten pages or a chapter a day.

We also have a post that goes out every morning in our group that is easy for everyone to see and use for self-improvement, affirmations, or motivation purposes. We also share tips that help people in their daily habits.

Unfortunately, I didn`t have access to any of that when I got started. So I did what I mentioned above and started with a blank document on my computer so that I could create my own systems. It was hard to duplicate because I wasn`t sure what I should be duplicating! I was essentially a customer for two years because I didn`t know what the right income-producing activities were. I showed up to every training, and I could get a couple of people interested, but I was never able to help them launch.

Now, I am known as a master recruiter, and I have helped hundreds of people learn how to be successful in network marketing. I learned what it actually meant to work on your business. I learned what was income-producing in network marketing. I learned how to create systems around what works.

The system of the influence

One of the best things you can do as you start your business is to create systems around social media. You can start to use different strategies to get the most out of these platforms. One of the biggest struggles I see people get into is not having a system to work these platforms. They start spinning and wasting their time thinking they are doing the business when all they are doing is mindlessly scrolling. Create a simple step-by-step system that can help you and your business builders utilize social media the right way. The best part about this and other systems is that they can grow as you grow.

Part of the social media system is going to be creating a community for your team. For years I have worked on creating a culture and community that aligned with my values of improvement and health. Now it is one of the strongest parts of our team. We also have a system where we have a monthly webinar for education and weekly business training. We answer questions, make recognition and announcements so that we can keep everyone up to date.

Do it messy. No system is perfect. I dare say it may never be. You can test and tweak it later, but just do it. You can launch with very little knowledge or systems when you're brand new. All you need is a slight awareness of the product. You are going on Facebook and doing a Facebook Live about the product. You could interview your upline. You could share your story. You can tell people why you are interested in starting your own business. I'm here to tell you that it won't be easy, and it may feel awkward at first, but you can do it anyway. The more you do any system, the better it will get.

Coach's Notes: If you and your teams don't have a social media system, your lack of system is the system. This means that everyone will look elsewhere at what to do. They will get confused. I still remember reading a quote from the author of *Think and Grow Rich*, **Napoleon Hill. "The number one cause of failure is indecision." We don't want our teams to be confused, so even if your social media system is simple, it still has huge value.**

If it isn't you, it's not for you

Remember what I told you in the beginning? Your systems will look different from other people`s systems because you do things differently. I wish I would have learned sooner to always be myself while growing my business. I remember thinking that I had to always wear a suit when I wouldn`t normally do that to be successful. I showed up uncomfortable and not being myself. I have always been different than others. I was that girl with the purple hair before the purple hair was cool! That was who I was, but I had limited myself to thinking that I had to "look the part to be successful." I was different, and I started to find great leads and people that wanted to work with me when I embraced my differences. It allowed other people that same space.

This goes for systems as well. Some people are really good at going and getting things done quickly and crushing it. Some people are very organized, and others are all over the place. I know for me, I have been both! But it never worked when I tried to put myself in another system that just wasn`t me. For the last two years, I`ve been mentored by a coach. The best part about the coaching has been embracing my way of doing systems. Because of that, I am being shown how to not only attract the right people but to get them into a habit of creating the good things in their lives that will make them happier, healthier, and wealthier. How great is that?!

You want to do business your way. You want to make sure that as you create systems, they are systems that you will go through with. If I told some people that they would have to personally meet with every single person that signed up with them, it would limit them. They could only meet with people personally, maybe they would only have certain times that they could meet, and maybe they wouldn't like meeting with people! That means the system of meeting people in person would HINDER their business, not help it. You will learn really quickly what works for you and what feels best for you.

Here are a couple of questions that will help you start to figure out exactly what systems you need to start to put in place for your business.

Are you a customer-based business? Will you be doing events online or in-person? How do people get their product after they have ordered it? How do you stay in touch with your customers? When does your introduction to the company, product, or business happen? If you have already been in business for a while, think back to what help you get customers. What follow-up did you use? What got them interested in the first place? How did they find you?

Conclusion

You need to know how you want to do business to start creating the systems. These questions above are an easy way to get started thinking about systems. When you have the right systems in place, you are positioning yourself for the win. You are focused on the long-term success of your business and using systems right now to make that happen.

Everything happens for a reason. I believe that today, the people who plan ahead plan to succeed. If in 2022, you are not grasping your life and creating a system out of it that can be flexible, and plan to review it, then you are wasting your time, and you aren't going to have the same results, if not worse, over and over and over. That is not how you want to live your life! Create systems that will help you live your best, Happy, Healthy, and Wealthy life. :)

Have a beautiful day, my friends.
Sonia Line Arseneau from New Brunswick, Canada.

Coach's Notes: I am a system guy for all aspects of my life. Sonia has found great success in systems. All businesses need systems. Franchises are attractive to business owners because of their systems. Never stop improving your systems in all aspects of your life and business.

> "You do not rise to the level of your goals. You fall to the level of your systems."
>
> — James Clear, *Atomic Habits*

SUE BRENCHLEY

- Thirty year full-time Network Marketing career.
- Married forty-seven years, four children, thirteen grandchildren.
- Earned over 10 million dollars in commissions.
- 7-figure income per year for over ten years.
- Passionate about serving others and suicide prevention.

Are you in "The Zone"?

We have all heard the phrase "In the zone," but what exactly is the zone, and how do you get in it?! There are several different zones that you may be familiar with. There is the comfort zone, the safety zone, land zones, and of course, time zones. I have found that several zones have helped me build my network marketing business that you are probably not familiar with. These zones have helped me through the journey of learning to love the process of finding those who are ready to embrace the kind of lifestyle that only this incredible profession can provide. I`m excited to share these zones, how to get in them, and the power they might provide you.

So what does it actually mean to "be in the zone"? According to the dictionary, it is being in a mental state of focused concentration on the performance of an activity. One dissociates oneself from distracting or irrelevant aspects of one`s environment. If you are in the zone, you are happy or excited because you are doing something very skillfully and easily.

It is also known as "being in a state of flow." In positive psychology, a flow state, also known colloquially as being in the zone, is the mental state in which a person performing some activity is fully immersed in a feeling of energized focus, full involvement, and enjoyment in the process of the activity.

Your goal should be to get into a flow and stay there as often as possible. This requires developing both your skills and your confidence. This will take time and practice, and learn to avoid spending too much time with people who aren`t interested in your products or ready for your opportunity. I hope you master the skill of recognizing which zone your prospect is in quickly to achieve the result that is in everyone`s best interest.

Coach's Notes: I am excited that Sue is going in-depth on this topic. She has attended so many masterminds and invested in herself repeatedly. This is even still when she is a top industry leader. As I read through her chapter, I smile because I am currently in a flow state. I have my phone off. I have all of my computer tabs closed. I am 100 percent present and focused on studying this chapter for myself and giving my insights on it to readers. Being in the flow state is the time hack to get more done faster.

Instability Zone

The instability zone is the most difficult and challenging zone to navigate. Many people we approach are in the instability zone, and although they need an opportunity, they might not be open. Some people want the opportunity of network marketing but are fearful of starting. These are the people who do not have the ability to purchase your product even though they "need" them. They are the people who just lost their job or had some other financial tragedy and need to become stable before they can participate in your opportunity or benefit from your products.

The people in the instability zone are in pain and are usually unable to look further into the future because they have to try and solve their pain. They are people who want more but are often in denial that they can embrace opportunity because it seems unreachable. You might even be in the instability zone yourself, and I want you to know that you can absolutely work your way out of it. The caution for you as you work with people in this zone is not to get stuck trying to fix people. Too often, we want to save someone in this zone and end up frustrated and discouraged. Prospects in this zone must desire to change their circumstances, be coachable, and be willing to work.

The secret to genuinely helping someone who is currently unstable financially is to make sure you are not overpromising what they can expect while keeping focused on their participation in getting trained and systematically taking action. Without committed engagement in the business, there is a high probability that they will give up and quit. Most people are capable of overcoming their current circumstances. However, it is wise to recognize the people who might not have the commitment to change.

As you work with your team, something to consider is, would you hire them if you were paying them a salary? There is a reason employers have a probationary period when they hire someone. Not everyone will succeed in your business, so love them all while working with those who work and produce results regardless of their zone.

Looking Zone

The next zone I call the looking zone. This is one of my favorite zones. I define the looking zone as the zone full of people looking for solutions to their problems and challenges. This zone is important because it helps us connect our solutions to other people`s problems. I have found that if you can connect with people and find out what they are looking for, you might just be in the position to help them solve their problems. That solution may be connected to your products, services, or opportunity. However, there are times that it may just be pointing them in another direction. The beauty of the looking zone is the ability to connect authentically with people in their needs or desires and make a difference in their situation.

I learned early in my career that network marketing is a people business. I`m so grateful for so many mentors who helped me understand that financial success in network marketing directly results in helping people succeed. Products fill a need and are often the solution people are looking for. However, the real power of our offering is the ability for average people to build a network of people-moving products, which improves their quality of life. A network of people who move products will result in solid companies that employ people and provide for families. More importantly, these networks of people focus on personal development as they grow and progress into amazing humans. As we learn to love people who are looking for friendship, acceptance, solutions to health or financial challenges, and sometimes just a kind and caring connection during a difficult time, we grow! The best part of

Network Marketing is helping as many people as you can and watching people improve their circumstances. When you are looking for people looking for what you have to offer and are ready and able to take action, you are in the best possible place to succeed.

To find people in the looking zone, there are several steps that are a must master. First, know what you are offering. You must have a basic knowledge of your product and business opportunity. This will help you know exactly what you bring to the market. Next, look for the problems that people are facing. These can be personal or professional. Finally, see your offer as the solution to everyone`s problem, and start making offers of help. Throughout your network marketing career, you will want to find people in the looking zone as quickly and as often as you can.

As you present your products and opportunities, you will soon find that the majority of your success will come from the people squarely in the middle of the looking zone. The real power of the looking zone is that most people are looking for something. If you can connect and offer the gift of what you have to as many as you can, you will find success over time and change lives.

Every day we have the opportunity to connect with people and serve them. In this zone, people are hungry to change their circumstances. If your prospect is open in this zone, they will experience the best of what this business is about. I think back to that moment over thirty years ago when I was open and looking for health solutions. I found products that would change my life and the knowledge that would allow me to dream about a better life and, over time, have those dreams come true.

I am grateful for the people who were open to sharing and embracing me during a difficult time in my life. Those people in my life were in the looking zone. They were able to teach me about a product that would never sell on a shelf because it needed someone to tell the story of its value, which was the solution to my problem. I hope you are starting to understand the power of the looking zone. We all pass through the looking zone where we are met by those ready and willing to share and serve. Sometimes that service or sharing of products results in a sale or transaction that benefits us financially though often it does not. If embraced, it will always result in a moment of growth and, at times, lifelong friendships.

As you learn to master being in the zone through mastering the art of service, you also need to know some secrets. First, spend time in the looking zone and don't focus outside of this zone when you are in it. Occasionally people will go below or above the looking zone, and they start to lose focus and get "out of the zone." In order to stay "in the zone," you have to be present there. Many people are tempted to spend their time looking outside the zone with little success and lots of disappointment. Don't get in the trap of being in one zone and wishing you were somewhere else. Be in the zone!

Belief Zone

Once you feel more confident and gain experience in this business, you will start to enter something I call the belief zone. You are starting to overcome some of your fears in the belief zone. You are starting to figure out who really wants help and how to help and connect more deeply with others. You are also starting to believe more in your product and company. Up to this point, you may have been borrowing beliefs from other people. You may have used other people's testimonials and been in the "hope it works" phase. As you move into the belief zone, you start having your own belief in the product, company, and yourself.

Often in this zone, I see people get into the flow of the business. They are learning what feels authentic to them. They are learning systems of getting people onboarded and how to step up and lead. They are starting to see success and believe that this may be the way to create the life and success they have always wanted. A couple of things that will help you get in the zone will be to work on your own story. Work on writing down your testimonial and what you love about network marketing. Don't let self-doubt or other people's judgments get you out of this zone. In the belief zone, you don't need to convince yourself or anyone else because you believe! The secret to moving from the belief zone to the success zone is mastering the skill of sorting and avoiding the need to convince.

Success Zone

The next zone is called the success zone. This is the space that is above the looking zone. The people in the success zone are focused. They have found what they were looking for and are in the process of growing. They focus on education, advancing their careers, living their healthiest lives, and even growing in their current network marketing company. People in the success zone have mastered the looking zone, and it has paid off by getting sales and are starting to get people interested in business opportunities.

One of the greatest things about the success zone is that it enables you to start to see the possibilities of this business for other people. On airplanes, they always talk about putting your oxygen mask on first before assisting other people. In the success zone, it's like you have secured your mask, and now you are ready to look around and see who else you can help.

This zone is where leadership starts to develop. You are not only helping people with a problem, but you are teaching them about the solution and how they can learn it and teach it as well. Duplication is key in the success zone. The better you show other people how to duplicate using systems, the more success you will have. Your goal: get in the success zone and stay there though others succeed,

There can be downsides to the success zone. Too often, people want these successful people in their organization and think to themselves: "If that person joined my business and brought their team, I would have made it." I have watched people approach a successful networker by telling them that they should start over with them because they have a better product. Not a great way to stay in the zone! The most important and respectful thing you can do if you are lucky enough to have the opportunity to associate with people in the success zone is simply to see if they will share their secrets and journey to success. If you have developed a relationship built on a foundation of respect, when they are in the looking zone, you will have their trust that could position you to work together when their current circumstances change.

Comfort Zone

This leads us to one last zone. The comfort zone. This zone can be the very thing that keeps us from success. The comfort zone was intended for us to take breaks and rest for short periods of time. It is the zone that holds us back from our full potential. It`s the zone that tells us that it`s enough or too hard or not worth the effort. It`s the place of settling when we are comfortable enough. As soon as you are comfortable with a skill, a rank, a paycheck, or anything you find comfortable, ask yourself, "what is next"?

The comfort zone will come and go in your business. As you learn and have more experience, you will get more comfortable. This is a great place to take a small break and then push yourself to the next level. Too often, I see people get stuck or want to stay in their comfort zone.

This will be the biggest factor in your success. If you want to continue growing and building your business, you want to only be in your comfort zone for short spurts of time. Instead of talking about getting into the zone for this, I want to share how to burst out of this zone.

First, use the comfort zone to rest and reset. Use the time to figure out what is next. Second, set a timeline. Don't find yourself hanging out here for too long. It's a lot like going on a vacation. Disneyland can be awesome, but not if you camp there too long! Last, focus on the next zone and what you want to accomplish. This will help you burst through the comfort zone.

Conclusion

Wherever you are right now, there is another level to achieve. We are stewards of products, knowledge, relationships, and purpose. We are incredibly blessed to live in a time of change and a time where more people than ever are in the looking zone. People who are looking for solutions.

People who are looking for you!

Coach's Notes: You will go in and out of different zones, and now you know them all. If you apply this knowledge, you will be able to shift up in zones more frequently. Applying this knowledge will teach this chapter to your current and future teams. Get in the ZONE, my friends. You don't lack time to have success, You lack focus.

CONCLUSION

I am blown away by the value that each of these authors added to their chapters. People pay tens of thousands of dollars to learn from these mentors, and they shared their wisdom with you here in their chapters. There was a lot of amazing information, and we don't want you to get stuck in information paralysis analysis. My challenge to you is to take one system or concept that you learned from these authors and create an action plan that you can start today.

This book will always be available to you and I want you to use it as a reference. If you ever find yourself stuck, or you are looking for the next step to take in your business, pull this book out and read one chapter. Find the tools to apply and then go out and take action.

The tools and concepts that we all shared are the best network marketing strategies in the world. But they only work if you put them to work! As you finish this book, I want you to go back to your notes. What can you implement right now? How are you going to utilize what you were taught and put into action immediately? When you are given the best network marketing strategies in the industry, it is up to you to make them work. Now go out and create success for yourself. At the beginning of this book I mentioned the HOW greed that you may experience as you get started. This book was FULL of all the HOW you would ever need to start your business and have success in network marketing. As you finish this book I want you to make a list of actionable steps that you are going to take this week! Notice that I didn't say this year, or this month. Take action fast and get working on your business. You need to stop preparing to prepare to prepare to get ready. Make the list and start taking action. You have got this!